01

The Work of
Christopher Wren

Frontispiece Sir Christopher Wren, 1632-1723.
Detail of marble bust by Edward Pierce (*c* 1635-95),
c 1673. *Ashmolean Museum, Oxford* (Photograph: Museum).
This spirited baroque bust was sculpted when Wren was
over 40 years old, and at a time when his mind was
preoccupied with the early designs and models for St Paul's
Cathedral. For the stance of the bust, *see* pl. 196.

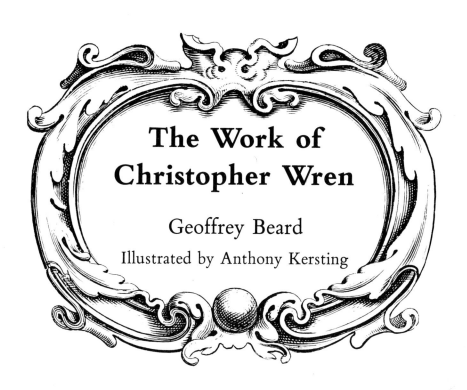

The Work of Christopher Wren

Geoffrey Beard

Illustrated by Anthony Kersting

John Bartholomew & Son Limited,
Edinburgh

First published in Great Britain 1982 by
John Bartholomew and Son Limited,
12 Duncan Street, Edinburgh EH9 1TA

**British Library Cataloguing in Publication
Data**
Beard, Geoffrey
The Work of Christopher Wren.
I. Wren, Sir Christopher
I. Title
720'.92'4   NA 997.W8

ISBN: 0 7028 8071 X

Printed in Edinburgh
by John Bartholomew & Son Limited.

Contents

Preface

In 1978, the 250th anniversary of the birth of the Scottish architect Robert Adam (1728-92) John Bartholomew and Son Ltd published my study of his work. The outstanding quality of the 60 colour and 180 black-and-white illustrations, mostly by Anthony Kersting, together with a short readable text, notes on each plate, chronology and bibliography ensured the book's success. It has now (1981) entered its third impression, and has encouraged the same team of author, photographer and publisher to attempt a similar format volume to commemorate the 350th anniversary of the birth of Sir Christopher Wren (1632-1723). Now, however, we were conscious of dealing with the national architect, and also with one London building, St Paul's Cathedral, which was known universally and which has been the scene of many important national events.

My own interest in Wren was stimulated in the early 1950s by many genial conversations, in his Putney house, with the late Professor Geoffrey Webb, himself the author of a most perceptive little book (1937) on Wren. I had been giving research help to Mrs Webb in her book (1954) on the sculptor, JM Rysbrack. Many meals took place in a room with Wren drawings on the walls, and these meetings with a splendid teacher combined information and reminiscence about Wren and Vanbrugh.

It is obvious, however, that this book does not seek to emulate any of the existing and valuable texts on Wren noted in the Bibliography. In varying degrees those by Sir John Summerson, the late Dr Margaret Whinney, Professor Kerry Downes and Drs Sekler and Fürst provide all that is necessary, and there is also the impressive back-up of 20 detailed volumes published by the Wren Society. I have used all these sources extensively and have thus been able to give considerable and merited attention to the craftsmen who worked under Wren's supervision. The relevant facts have been put alongside a greater range of illustrations than has hitherto appeared in any single volume on Wren's work.

For these illustrations it is obvious that I am indebted mainly to Anthony Kersting, whose files already included many valuable pre-war photographs of St Paul's and the City churches. With his customary application, however, and with the ready help of the Dean and Chapter of St Paul's Cathedral, the First Lieutenant of the Royal Naval

College, Greenwich, and of church, university and public officials he provided many new photographs of unfailing quality.

For help of various kinds I am grateful to the Dean and Chapter of St Paul's Cathedral and to the Receiver, Cdr Charles Shears, RN; the Warden and Fellows of All Souls College, Oxford; Sir John Summerson and Miss Dorothy Stroud (Sir John Soane's Museum, London); David Dean (The British Architectural Library); John Kerslake (National Portrait Gallery); Stephen Croad (National Monuments Record); the Sub-Warden of St Deiniol's Library, Hawarden; the photographic staffs of the Courtauld Institute of Fine Art, University of London and of the University of Lancaster; the print room staff of the Guildhall Library, London; Robert Boumphrey; Nicholas and Judith Goodison; Margaret Knapp; and my wife and daughter.

Geoffrey Beard

University of Lancaster
September 1981

I

'Miracle of a Youth'

At Oxford 'where after dinner I visited that
miracle of a youth, Mr. Christopher Wren'

John Evelyn, *Diary,* 10 July 1654'[1]

On 20 October 1632 a delicate child was born at the village rectory of East Knoyle, Wiltshire to the Revd Dr Christopher Wren and his wife Mary. Like his father, and an earlier son who had died young, he was to be named Christopher. This 'second Christopher', who was to make the name of Wren so famous, was reared in the High Church tradition along with several sisters. In 1634 Wren's father, who was a mathematician with some knowledge of drawing and architecture, was appointed to succeed his brother Matthew as Dean of Windsor. He had been one of the King's chaplains since 1628, and took up with equal energy his brother's role, which carried with it the registrarship of the Order of the Garter. Thus it was that Christopher Wren as a precocious young boy came to live at the sombre edge of historic surroundings of the Caroline court. Few had reason to assume at this point that he would live to be over ninety years old, become Surveyor of the King's Works, serve as an eminent scientist and astronomer, and become the architect, in particular, of St Paul's Cathedral in London.

Dr Wren seems to have divided his residence among Windsor, Great Haseley, near Oxford (to which living he had been presented by King Charles I), and from 1646 the even more tranquil setting of Bletchington in Oxfordshire. The King asked him to estimate for a building at Windsor to be used by the Queen. The designs and specifications of its banqueting room, galleries and rooms for the Lord Chamberlain and court officials were probably the first concerns with architecture which came to young Christopher Wren's attention. His delicate health was the cause of much anxiety to his busy father and his sister Susan. But as with many weakly children he studied hard and passed on from the care of his tutor, in his ninth or tenth year, to Westminster School. Westminster was then under the rule of its famous headmaster Dr Richard Busby. During the same period Christopher's mathematical tutor was Dr William Holder, who had married the sixteen year old Susan Wren in 1643, and was thus his brother-in-law. Holder, a friend of Thomas Hobbes, was sub-dean of the Chapel Royal, and a canon residentiary of St Paul's and of Ely.

In an early letter of 1641 written in Latin and addressed to his father *(see* pl. 193) Wren had indicated to 'Venerande Pater' that 'what in me lies I will perform, as much as I am able ...'. When he was fourteen he left Westminster School and went up to

Oxford as a Gentleman Commoner at Wadham College. He distinguished himself at Westminster, by inventing in 1645 an astronomical instrument. He possessed that kind of enquiring mind which could concern itself with the new experimental philosophy. When Wren went up to Oxford it was not only the seat of the University, but also of the Royalist Court as the King was in refuge there. In the midst of these differing influences Christopher was able to pursue his studies under the care of Dr John Wilkins, later Bishop of Chester. John Evelyn, (later Wren's life-long friend) called him 'the most obliging and universally curious Dr Wilkins'. He was devoted to experiments, and was the author of a book *A Discovery of a New World,* concerning the unknown art of flying. He was an able teacher and it was probably due to the fact that he was married to Cromwell's sister that saved Wadham College, when Oxford capitulated to the forces of General Thomas Fairfax on 24 June 1646.

Also resident at Wadham College at this time was the learned philosopher and mathematician, Dr Seth Ward, and the no less celebrated William Oughtred, the most eminent mathematician of his day. In the company of eminent men, and gratified by the fact that Dr Wilkins had introduced him as a prodigy in science to Prince Charles, Elector Palatine, Wren flourished intellectually, but was still weak in health. Sir Charles Scarborough, a friend of Dean Wren's, and then rising to fame as a surgeon not only cared for him when he was ill, but used him as a demonstrating assistant at Surgeons' Hall, and induced him, before he was out of his teens, to undertake the translation into Latin of Oughtred's *Clavis Mathematicae* (1652). This was a treatise of great reputation on mechanical dialling. That his translation satisfied Oughtred is evident from the Latin preface in which the author wrote of:

Mr Christopher Wren, Gentleman Commoner of Wadham College, a youth generally admired for his talents, who, when was not yet sixteen years old, enriched astronomy, gnomonics, static and mechanics, by brilliant inventions, and from that time has contributed to enrich them, and in truth is one from whom I can, not vainly, look for great things.[2]

The talents Oughtred praised led Wren through his Bachelor's degree in 1650 and he was almost ready for any profession. The following three years before taking his Master's degree (1653) were filled with intense activity. Wren was recorded in 1650 as being the first inventor of the micrographic art; that of drawing enlarged views of subjects as they appeared through a microscope. In these attempts he was assisted by Robert Hooke, who afterwards issued an account of their discoveries under the title of *Micrographia* (1665).[3] It remained in Wren's library, along with works by Newton, Huygens, Evelyn, Boyle and Wallis until the auction of its varied contents in October 1748. The road to fame and eminence was undertaken by the route which led from boy philosopher and astronomy professor to architect. That he was able to do experiments to prove the Harvey hypothesis of the circulation of blood, argue theories on the planet Saturn, write algebraical treatises on the Julian period, invent a diplographic instrument for writing with two pens, and compose metrical essays in Latin were extraordinary talents to which was added a growing skill in the art of design. To John Evelyn he was 'that miracle of a youth, Mr Christopher Wren' and in August 1657 recognition of his talents came when he succeeded Laurence Rooke as Professor of Astronomy at Gresham College in London.

Wren's inaugural oration, *(see* pl. 195) delivered in Latin, was addressed to the learned audience whose deliberations and experiments were to attract, eventually, the patronage of Charles II and lead to the foundation of the Royal Society. The lecturer owned, modestly, that before an assembly in which 'I spy some of the politer genii of our age' he wished to explain 'what hath been delivered to us by the ancients, concerning the motions and appearances of the celestial bodies ...'.[4] After the inaugural oration, which at once established his reputation, the young professor continued his lectures on astronomy at Gresham College every Wednesday in term time, 'attended by the same company of eminent and learned persons, who were with the auditors of Mr Rooke, his predecessor'.[5] The Oxford society or 'the Club' who were all Wren's friends gathered at the Gresham lectures, and were joined by a group from London who had similar scientific pursuits and inclinations.

In May 1658 Wren had to contend with the melancholy arising from the death of his father but the occasions for meeting in the company of friends allowed him to tackle a problem set 'to the learned of England' by Jean de Monfert, a fictitious name assumed by Blaise Pascal, the French mathematician and philosopher.[6] It was to be solved by a given day, and Wren's solution, printed in 1658, and which in turn propounded another problem taken from Kepler, was studied carefully by the French mathematicians. They remained silent as to its validity and avoided paying the promised prize of twenty pistoles. It provided indirectly the soundness of Wren's mathematical learning, as he had solved the Kepler problem, on which the French had likewise been silent. Although the discovery of a straight line equal to a cycloid and its parts, the theories of refraction, and the improvement of optical instruments were all set out in other Gresham lectures, the texts are lost. What was not in doubt, in the troublous period as Cromwell died, and when thoughts of the King's return from France could be entertained covertly, was Wren's reputation as a brilliant and practical scientist.

Gresham College, occupied by soldiers in the short interlude of 1658-59 when Richard Cromwell had succeeded his father in the Protectorship, was no longer a conducive place for learning; Wren's friend, Bishop Sprat, had written to him of the soldiers' crime, 'since by hindering your lecturers they have committed so manifest a mischief against Heaven'.[7] John Evelyn avoided working for the Commissioners of New Buildings because he did not want to take an oath of fidelity to the Government. The times were not favourable to the progress of science, but in the way that Sir Robert Shirley had indicated over the porch of Staunton Harold Church, Leicestershire, built during the Commonwealth, that he did the 'best things in the worst time' so did the desire for knowledge, and particularly of natural and experimental philosophy, increase. The setting up of a regular society was uppermost in the thoughts of Wren and other distinguished company. The astronomy professor was also studying chemistry, at Oxford along with Robert Boyle and the German chemist, Peter Sthael of Strasbourg. It was the year which John Evelyn called 'Annus Mirabilis' - 1660 - in which the diarist noted that the restoration of a monarchical government had been possible without bloodshed. A few days before the King's restoration Wren succeeded Dr Seth Ward (afterwards Bishop of Salisbury) as Savilian Professor of Astronomy at Oxford.

The restoration of the King gave England a confidence it had lacked in the previous troubled decades. The purpose of the founders of the Royal Society was, as Bishop Sprat noted, 'to make faithful records of all the works of nature or art which can come within their reach ...' and to lay 'a philosophy of mankind'.[8] Wren was a brilliant example of their intention, and was identified not only with the setting-up of the original structure, but as a noticeable advocate of a royal charter. After the Gresham lecture of 5 December 1660, Sir Robert Moray brought the welcome news to Wren and thirty-eight illustrious friends that the King had approved of their regular meeting, and indeed was ready to encourage them. The group had Wren as a focal point, with his preparation of papers on the pendulum, shipping, the construction of solar eclipses, and of longitude and the instruments for determining it. The whole of Wren's discoveries, inventions and works may never be recovered. He was careless of present fame, and printed little himself. It was claimed in the family chronicle *Parentalia*[9] that he complained sharply that his inventions and papers were often sent abroad, where they were claimed by others.

The King however recognised Wren's worth and commanded letters to be sent to him at All Souls College, 'that his majesty expects you should prosecute your design of making representation of the lunar globe in *solido* and that you should proceed in drawing the shapes of little animals as they appear in the microsocope ...'.[10] The globe, fashioned into a true model of the moon was fixed upon a handsome pedestal of *lignum vitae* and with a resounding Latin dedication was presented to the King. Its author was now a Doctor of Civil Law of both Oxford and Cambridge, and with the members of the newly incorporated Royal Society he was to wait eventually upon the King at Whitehall to thank him for the patent of their establishment. The King had known of the loyalty of Wren and his family during the Commonwealth, and being also aware of his growing concern with architectural design invited him from Oxford to London. Through his cousin Matthew, son of Wren's uncle, the Bishop of Ely and then Secretary to Lord Clarendon, the King offered Wren the 'commission to survey and direct the works of the mole, harbour and fortifications of the citadel and town of Tangier'. If he would go out there he would be offered the reversion of Sir John Denham's Surveyorship of the King's Works.[11]

Tangier had come to Britain as part of the dowry of Catherine of Braganza, and as one of the best geometricians in Europe Wren was selected to be offered the appointment. There was still no distinct body of professional knowledge in architecture and engineering. The practical traditional skill of a mason or carpenter was bound fast in tradition and precedent. To accomplish more required ability in the mathematical sciences. It was an impressive gesture of confidence in Wren's accomplishments, but he declined it on the grounds of his health. It may well be, that in asking His Majesty 'to command his duty in England'[12] he saw a less spectacular but fascinating architectural problem arising in his beloved Oxford.

References and notes

1 Evelyn J. *Diary.* De Beer E S, ed. Oxford: Clarendon Press, 1955: Vols 1-6.

2 Oughtred W. *Clavis Mathematicae.* Oxford: T Robertson, 1652.

3 Hooke R. *Micrographia.* London: J Martyn & J Allestry, 1665.

4 The text of the 1657 inaugural lecture is given, In: Wren S. *Parentalia, or memoirs of the Family of Wrens.* London: T Osborn & R Dodsley, 1750 *(see Bibliography - Wren S.)* and In: Elmes J. *Memoirs of the Life and Works of Sir Christopher Wren.* London, 1823 Appendix 9:40-53.

5 Ward J. *The lives of the Professor of Gresham College,* London, 1740:96

6 Some of Wren's correspondence with Pascal on the subject of their disputations was published, In: *Literae ad D Pascal.* Paris, 1658.

7 Sprat Bishop T. *The History of the Royal Society of London.* London: J R for J Martyn, 1667:58.

8 *Ibid:* 8.

9 Wren S. *Op cit* (4) and *see* Bibliography.

10 *Ibid:* 209.

11 *Ibid:* 250n. *Parentalia* dates the King's letter in 1663 but a reference in it to Dr Baylie as Vice-Chancellor of Oxford University dates it to 1661-62 *cf* Colvin H M, ed. *History of the King's Works, 1660-1782.* London: HMSO, 1978; **V:** 16.

12 Cunningham A. *The lives of the most eminent British Painters, Sculptors and Architects.* London: John Murray, 1831; **IV:** 172-173.

II

'Our English Vitruvius'

'contrived by our English Vitruvius, the Right
Worshipful and Learned Sir Christopher Wren'.

Robert Plot on the Sheldonian Theatre at
Oxford, *Natural History
of Oxfordshire*, 1677.[1]

Oxford

In the aftermath of the siege of Oxford in 1648 the Warden of All Souls College, Gilbert Sheldon, had been expelled. He was able to return twelve years later at the Restoration, and was soon elevated as Bishop of London. He wanted to make a grand leaving present to the University in the form of a classical building in which the new Masters of Arts could be created. On 29 April 1663 Wren showed a model of the Sheldonian Theatre to the Royal Society. A fortnight later on 13 May 1663 the Master of Pembroke College, Cambridge laid the foundation stone of the new chapel, also designed by Wren. They were his first architectural works. Fittingly the endowment for the Cambridge building came from his uncle Matthew, who on his release from eighteen years of imprisonment in the Tower employed his nephew as architect of his gift to his former college. They were the years which turned the scientist - astronomer into an accomplished architect, with these early achievements in Oxford, Cambridge and London.

Sheldon, as the new Bishop of London, also had the considerable problem of restoring the damaged Gothic pile of Old St Paul's Cathedral. As early as 1661 he asked Wren to consider what could be done to a church which had been patched and altered on four significant occasions since the original Norman building. It was a task which hindered the pursuit of astronomy, and from Oxford Bishop Sprat wrote to Wren in 1663 and said that he had been sent for by the Vice-Chancellor 'to inquire where the astronomy professor was, and the reason for his absence, so long after the beginning of the term ...'.[2] Sprat indicated that he had given as reasons 'for your defence' the demands of the King, the rebuilding of St Paul's and the fortification of Tangier; although the Vice-Chancellor was less than satisfied, Wren held the Savilian Professorship until 1673.

His first major building however, the Sheldonian Theatre in Oxford (*see* pls. 4-9, 61-62), was more of a practised mathematical exercise than an architectural triumph. The building as erected was without precedent in England, and Wren's achievement in roofing over the interior structure without using interior columns was notable. Dr Robert Plot in his *Natural History of Oxfordshire* (1677),[3] gave an excellent description of its construction; saying that it had been contrived by 'our English Vitruvius'. Plot's account, and his illustration of the roof structure (*see* pls. 7-8) were technical statements, and may have well have been obtained from Wren himself. For his plan the architect had turned to antiquity, seemingly basing some of his thoughts and design on the Theatre of Marcellus (*see* pl. 6) which he knew through the treatise by Sebastiano Serlio, titled *Architettura*. This had been published in various editions from 1537 and was given an English translation in 1611.[4] Wren's library catalogue shows that he owned the Venice edition of 1663.

Roman theatres, suited admirably to display and spectacle were however open to the sky, or protected from the sun by a *velarium* or awning. This was of no use in a rain-swept Britain, and as the building was more than 20 metres (70 feet) wide no single beam of wood could span the width. Wren was assisted by the researches of his Oxford friend, John Wallis, and the carpenter Richard Frogley in devising a solution based on such technical considerations. Serlio had shown how large spans could be covered by beams which were set into truss form, in which the triangular sloping sides carried the roof and its flat base, spliced together where necessary, held the ceiling. Plot went on to indicate that in imitation of ancient theatres a twisted 'rope', fashioned from oak, was inserted under the painted ceiling to simulate those which supported the early awnings. The whole interior was finished with paintings by the Sergeant Painter, Robert Streeter. Samuel Pepys, in his diary (1 February 1669) wrote:

to Mr Streeter's the famous history painter, over the way, whom I have often heard of, but never did see him before; and there I found him, and Dr Wren, and several Virtuosos, looking upon the paintings which he is making for the new Theatre at Oxford; and indeed they look as if they would be very fine...

Despite all his architectural distractions Wren still found time to assist his Oxford friend, Dr Thomas Willis, The Sedleian Professor of Natural Philosophy, in his anatomical description of the brain. The accurate drawings by Wren appeared in Willis's *Cerebri anatome* (1664),[5] one of a number of publications which kept the Royal Society ahead of its rival in Paris, the Academie Royale des Sciences, established by Louis XIV in February 1663. As for Wren, he kept ahead of most by his new perspective instrument, his weather-clock (*see* pl 194), and by applying his mind to such phenomena as observing the passing of the planet Mercury over the sun with an inverted tube or telescope. After telling the Royal Society late in 1664 that being a benefactor to mankind was best effected by advancing knowledge, profit, health and conveniences of life, Wren turned to his work as architect to Trinity College, Oxford, and to preparations for his first journey abroad.

At Trinity College, the President was Wren's friend, Dr Ralph Bathurst, who had studied chemistry with him under Peter Sthael. Dr Bathurst was also a poet who wrote in Latin, a distinguished wit and one of the most eminent men in English literature. Wren was preparing designs for the north-west wing of the garden quadrangle (1668), but wrote to Bathurst on 22 June 1665 that the site was not ideal, and that if he could not make the benefactors of his opinion 'I will appeal to Mons. Mansard, or Signor Bernini, both which I shall see at Paris within this fortnight'.[6]

Wren's important visit to Paris, his only known visit to the Continent, was made before he presented drawings for the repair of Old St Paul's (on which he had been asked to advise in 1663). Too little is known of the visit but Wren journeyed to Paris with a letter of introduction to Henry Jermyn, Earl of St Albans, the English ambassador. Lord St Albans had lived at Paris in great ease and luxury during the Rebellion, to a far greater degree more so than the King, to John Evelyn's disgust. He was a virtuoso and wit, and had considerable influence with the Queen Dowager, Henrietta Maria. He entertained Wren with courtesy and hospitality, and was later to be his patron at the building of St James's, Westminster (1682-84).

Much of what Wren did in Paris is obscure, but some of his activities he recorded in a letter written for the Revd Dr Bateman, the friend who had introduced him to the Earl of St Albans. Therein he noted that he had busied himself 'in surveying the most esteemed Fabricks of Paris, and the country around'. It is certain he met the elderly Bernini, indicating that the design of the Louvre 'I would have given my skin for, but the old reserv'd Italian gave me but a few minutes View'. He was fascinated by the reorganisation of the Louvre under Colbert, and he also acquired many French engravings.

The designs for Old St Paul's, presented soon after Wren's return, early in 1666, show a proposal to replace the central tower with a dome, derived in part from the Church of the Sorbonne, and to create a broad form of piazza. The destruction of Old St Paul's along with much of the City of London in the Great Fire of September 1666 rendered the design useless. The idea of dome and piazza lingered on however in Wren's retentive mind, as did the great palatial *cours d'honneur* of Richelieu, the Palais Royal and Versailles. They reappeared with variations in Wren's first designs for Greenwich, for Hampton Court and for Winchester Palace. French influence also formed the detailing of the porch of the City church of St Mary le Bow, taken from Mansart's Hôtel Conti in Paris (*see* pl 154), and the transept detailing of St Paul's from Mansart's design for the east elevation of the court of the Louvre in Paris.

On the night of 2 September 1666, there began, near Fish Street in the City, what has been called emphatically the *Great Fire* of London. John Evelyn described the conflagration in his diary with the fevered accuracy of an eye-witness who felt deeply the catastrophe of the burning metropolis:

... as it burned both in breadth and length, The Churches, Publique Halls, Exchange, Hospitals, Monuments & ornaments, leaping after a prodigious manner from house to house & streete to streete ...[8]

It was the Fire which, following the ravages of plague which the Royal Society had studied so carefully, gave Wren his great opportunity. He was appointed one of the three Royal Commissioners for the rebuilding of the city, and stood at the threshold of being appointed Surveyor-General of the King's Works.

On 4 March 1669 Sir John Denham, then ill, and with his position as Surveyor-General soon to be at the King's disposal, wrote to Lord Arlington. He indicated that by the terms of his Patent he had power to make a deputy, and that the King's wish (intimated by the Duke of Buckingham) was that Dr Christopher Wren be appointed. Sir John desired a warrant to be obtained, and said that he knew of no verbal deputations from Hugh May (1622-84) - one of the contenders for the post at his appointment - or anyone else. He further stated that if they had indeed made representation it was without his consent. John Webb (1611-72) had petitioned the King as early as 2 May 1660 for the post. He had been brought up by Inigo Jones, had married Jones's niece, and was one of the Commissioners to regulate building in London, and at Jones's death in 1652 had been left almost without a rival in the architectural field. He could, in the words of his petition 'discharge the said trust to yor Honors good satisfaction and the best advantage of the State'.[9] Webb thought little of Denham, pouring scorn on his 'possible' ability in architecture, having perhaps in mind that he was, as John Evelyn also stated, 'a better poet than architect'.[10] What he overlooked was that Denham had lent the King money during the long exile.

As Denham was ill Webb pressed his case hard. He said that he did not mind working under Denham, 'a person of honour', and that he only wished to be joined in patent with Wren so that he could instruct him in Office of Works procedures of which Wren professed to be ignorant. Denham's recommendation, aided by the King's own percipience in noting early the 'miracle of a youth' (as Evelyn called Wren) won the day, and on 28 March 1669, following Denham's death, Wren was appointed Surveyor-General of the King's Works. What neither Wren, Webb or May realised was that the candidates also numbered Sir Roger Pratt, Sir Robert Hooke, Sir Thomas Chicheley, (who opposed Wren over the proposal to put a dome on St Paul's) and the City Surveyor, Edward Jarman. The post brought Wren into closer contact with the King and Queen, the Privy Council and the Lords of the Treasury. Perhaps as compensation Hugh May was made Controller of the Works at Windsor Castle.

The main properties which were maintained structurally by the Office of Works were those in Whitehall, and the Royal residences at St James's, Windsor, Hampton Court and Kensington, the Parliament buildings around Westminster; during Wren's regime the buildings at Greenwich, Chelsea, Audley End and Newmarket were also supervised. In a system where countless hands were engrossing a mass of detail into the great Works' ledgers it was necessary to formulate exact rules of procedure. These in short cross-checked, and allocated responsibility for the sums of money being expended on legitimate repairs and renewals. The early years of Charles II's reign were spent by Wren and his officials in tussling with the enormous problems which lay in the wake of the Plague and Great Fire. The city had to be rebuilt.

References and notes

[1] Plot R. *Natural History of Oxfordshire.* Oxford: The Theatre, 1677.

[2] Sprat Bishop T. The text of this letter is given in *Parentalia. Op cit:* 201 and In: Elmes J. *Op cit:* 111-112.

[3] Plot R. *Op cit:* 274. *See* pls. 7-8.

[4] Serlio S. *The first booke of Architecture.* London: E Stafford, 1611. A cautionary note on Wren's use of Serlian motifs is given by Viktor Fürst, *Op cit:* 129 (*see* Bibliography). Sir John Summerson, *Op cit:* (*see* Bibliography) notes the form of loaded beams given in Serlio and studied by John Wallis, one of Wren's Oxford friends, and like him a Savilian Professor (of Geometry) in the University.

[5] Wren C. Drawings. In: Willis T. *Cerebri anatome.* London, 1664.

[6] Wren's letter to Dr Bathurst. In: Bolton A T, Hendry H D, eds. *The Wren Society.* London, 1924-43: **XIII**: 40-41

[7] *Ibid.* But *see* Whinney M D. Sir Christopher Wren's Visit to Paris. *Gazette des Beaux Arts* 1958: **L1**: 229-242.

[8] Evelyn J. *Diary. Op. cit,* 1666 Sept 3.

[9] Bolton A T, Hendry H D, eds. *Op cit:* **XVIII**: 12

[10] Evelyn J. *Diary. Op. cit,* 1661 Oct 19.

The London City Churches

In 1673 Wren resigned his position as Savilian Professor of Astronomy at Oxford, as his architectural career was absorbing most of his time. In the busy years after the Great Fire he concerned himself particularly with the City Churches, and, as the 1670s advanced, with St Paul's and the Royal Palaces. By a combination of acumen and ability Wren had turned himself from a competent amateur in architecture to a master of complicated designs, and intricate spatial organisation. His assistant, as one of the three surveyors appointed to rebuild the churches, was Robert Hooke, who recorded in his diary that he received his salary 'on City Churches account'.[1] He also jotted down the many occasions on which he dined with his celebrated friend, and commented on the scientific and intellectual pursuits they undertook.

In *Parentalia* it is stated that Hooke's duty respecting the churches was to survey the sites, but the many payments to others for this precise and boring task belies the statement. With Wren or Edward Woodroffe, the third surveyor, he visited the churches often in the course of their construction. It also seems very likely that he prepared many of the drawings for the churches, or had a significant hand in them. He overlooked most of the contracts and agreements with the teams of craftsmen, and occasionally (as for St Stephen, Walbrook) passed the accounts instead of Wren. Hooke also had his own small but important architectural practice, and he collaborated with Wren in designing the Monument (*see* pls. 43, 144) in 1673.

The complex administration needed to supervise so many individual church rebuildings - 87 had been destroyed and 52 were rebuilt - may be gauged from the fact that 17 were started in 1670, and by 1676, when Wren was also much involved with St Paul's, 28 were in hand. The surveyors had to reckon too, with the individual comments and demands of each Vestry. Wren would submit a plan and Hooke and Woodroffe (d. 1675) would visit the sites, talk to the Vestry officers, and supervise the craftsmen. So while Wren's share in the evolution of the designs was crucial, he had considerable help in their execution. It is now difficult to see exactly what he did, and there is much that is well below his own standard, and is aesthetically unsatisfactory. The churches were also much altered in the 18th and 19th centuries, and damaged extensively in the Second World War. Nineteenth century demolitions, changes in population and conversion to other purposes went alongside the rich displays of Victorian stained glass, and heavy colour schemes. The surviving accounts (Bodleian Library), show that wainscoted and light stone-coloured or white interiors, with clear glass, were the architect's intention. The greatest interest of the churches lies in the variety of interior plan, and the towers and steeples soaring over crowded streets.

The plans fall into two main types: traditional oblong buildings with nave and aisles; and small square buildings with the space arranged in a variety of ways. The large oblongs often have plastered barrel-vaults (as St Bride, Fleet Street, *see* pl. 158), with galleries above the side aisles, and, formed of five bays, owe something to the Vitruvius basilica. The smaller churches demonstrate the architect's ingenuity in deriving satisfactory and interesting spaces for difficult sites. St Antholin, St Benet Fink, and St Mary Abchurch, (*see* pl. 143) show the experiments with elliptical dome shapes. The obsession with controlling the forms of geometry was applied at its most extreme in the plan of St Benet Fink - a decagon, with six columns holding up the dome.

In *Parentalia*[2] it was noted that Wren's intention was to rebuild 'all the Parish Churches in such a Manner as to be seen at the End of a Vista of Houses, and dispersed in such Distances from each other, as to appear neither too thick, nor thin in Prospect' but this did not happen. The sites, as we have noted, were cramped and awkward, and no grand baroque piazzas were possible. There was also a need to conform to Protestant liturgy with congregations able to observe and participate, rather than to imagine, in a Romish setting, the distant incense-wreathed elevation of the Host. The point must not be laboured, however, for the missionary zeal of the Jesuits and their influence on church design was widening participation by their congregations.

In order to erect the new churches with decent haste the foundations of the medieval churches were often used. Hooke's extensive architectural library, and indeed Wren's own, were ransacked for ideas, and French and Dutch influences (St Anne and St Agnes, St Martin, Ludgate) apart from Serlian motifs, can be discerned. The fascinating question of Wren's sources is touched on again in the final chapter, but has been examined in great detail in two books by Eduard Sekler[3] and Viktor Fürst.[4] Nicholas Hawksmoor, Wren's talented assistant in his late years, noted that the body of the church of St Mary-le-Bow (*see* pl. 139) was derived from the Temple of Peace, a Roman building better known as the Basilica of Maxentius, and published in Serlio and other sources. A copy of *Vitruvius* was also bought for the Wren office in 1676.

The Bow tower steeple and lantern (*see* pl. 139) facing on to Cheapside, and with a doorway at the base of the tower is a rich and complex invention, based on François Mansart's design for the doorway of the Hôtel de Conti in Paris (*see* pls. 153-154), but with different proportions. Begun in 1671 it starts as a square tower, topped by a belfry with round-headed windows, and coupled Ionic pilasters at each corner. Elaborate scrolls above the balustrade bear urns, and lead the eye upwards over a colonnaded circular temple-like structure to the twelve inverted brackets which carry the Corinthian-columned lantern. Finally a tall pyramid carries a ball and a weathervane in the form of a dragon. This was designed in 1680 by Edward Pierce, the sculptor of the splendid bust of Wren (*see* pls. 90,196). He made a model to aid the bronze-caster, and also one to establish that the size was in scale to the whole.

These steeples on Wren churches are usually later in date than the main body of the buildings they adorn. Two of the finest, the baroque steeple of St Vedast (*see* pl. 137), and the lantern of St Magnus The Martyr (*see* pl. 151) are dated 1697 and 1705 respectively. Wren compiled a Memorandum about 1711 giving his views on the churches in the east and west of the City to be erected under an Act of 1708. He wrote of 'handsome spires, or Lanterns, rising in good Proportion above the neighbouring Houses' and where there were open spaces', of church fronts adorned with porticoes (*see* pl. 181).[5] That of St Dunstan-in-the-East (*see* pl. 146) recreated the medieval 'corona' of old St Mary-le-Bow. Others were successful by their piercing lancet form (*see* pls 149, 172), or controlled build-up of effect through several stages, as at St Bride's, Fleet Street, (*see* pl. 157) and Christ Church, Newgate Street (*see* pls. 176, 178).

In some final late forms it was Borromini's church of S Ivo della Sapienza in Rome that gave inspiration to setting small columned steeples above a tower. That of St Michael, Paternoster Royal, St James, Garlick Hill and St Stephen, Walbrook were all variations on this theme (*see* pls. 162, 174). The late Dr Margaret Whinney also noted the Pieter Huyssens Church of St Charles Borremo in Antwerp as the source for the design of St Magnus The Martyr with its octagonal steeple and cupola (*see* pl. 151) above a square tower. Their forms acted as a foil to the bulk of St Paul's Cathedral, and captivated the topographical artists (*see* pls. 138, 147).

Next in importance were the internal fittings - the pulpits, (*see* pls. 167, 170), the richly carved altars (*see* pl. 166) and organ-cases (*see* pl. 183), and the well-beaten white and gilded plasterwork. The craftsmen of these fittings were engaged for the most part in work on Royal Palaces, and owed allegiance to the Office of Works, but were able to take on private commissions as they arose. This led to much invention and coarse execution, from which the mind and eye of the architect were absent. It also led to some achievements of rare quality, if a robust vitality could be condoned (*see* pl. 180).

St Mary-le-Bow, along with St Lawrence Jewry (*see* pl. 141) and St Stephen, Walbrook (*see* pls. 142, 173) were the most costly and important of the first group of churches. As St Stephen's an ingenious plan set a dome on a rectangular base, through the use of eight equal arches. The insertion of windows at various well-chosen points flooded the interior with light. The thrust upwards through the Corinthian columns contrasted with the dark box-pews (since replaced) which reached the height of the pedestals supporting the columns. With its rich carved fittings, donated by the Grocers' Company, partly discernible in an early engraving (*see* pl. 173) it provided a most accomplished interior.

Some of the churches were built from the steady revenues derived from the coal tax, but others came through subscriptions and private support. St Andrew's Holborn, St Clement Danes (with its later spire added by James Gibbs, *see* pls. 184-185), and St James's, Piccadilly were erected in this way. St James's was erected at the expense of the Lord St Albans, whom Wren had met in Paris, and who was developing his estates in the West End. They are all aisled churches with galleries (*see* pl. 183), and when Wren compiled the Memorandum, already referred to, he singled out St James's for special mention as an economical and spacious interior - 'I think it may be found beautiful and convenient, and as such, the cheapest of any Form I could invent'.[6]

Wren's intentions in the City churches of the 1670s are now well summarised in the interior of St James, Garlick Hill (or Garlickhythe). The aisles have flat ceilings, with clerestory windows set above the columns in the nave. The Victorian windows shown (*see* pl. 163) have been replaced with clear glass, and much of its woodwork is intact. There was occasional variation in the number of aisles. St Lawrence Jewry, where a pedimented east end gives the elevation added distinction (*see* pl. 141) has one aisle on the north side, and St Benet (now the Welsh Church) also has only one aisle. Here a rare use of brick with garlands above the windows, and stone quoins at the corners shows Dutch influence (*see* pl. 160). This may have been derived from books in Hooke's library, such as those by Philip Vingboons, who also had an effect on English domestic architecture during the Commonwealth.

The centralised form of church plan, important to Renaissance architects, was never far from Wren's own thoughts. St Mary Abchurch, started in 1681 was given a shallow dome set over an almost square plan. The dome however was not painted until after 1708 when it was done in oil on plaster, either by Isaac Fuller II or William Snow, with a scene of angels making music and adoring the Hebrew name of God (*see* pl. 143). A feigned stone cornice is pierced by four oval windows. At St Swithin, Cannon Street (*see* pl. 179), destroyed in 1941, an eight-sided dome covered the body of the church, and we have noted the decagon of St Benet, with its oval dome on six columns.

The knowledge Wren gained on building the City churches he was able to use in the early stages of St Paul's. The churches also acted as important training grounds for the masons, sculptors, plasterers and carvers, many of whom worked on St Paul's for the rest of their lives. They overcame shortages of money and materials and surmounted the problems inherent in building at some 50 congested sites. They act as the safe touchstone for assessing the brilliance and pragmatic abilities of the Surveyor-General, now intent in the demands set by the rising structure of St Paul's.

References and notes

[1] Hooke R. *Diary 1672-80.* Robinson H W, Adams W, eds. London: Taylor & Francis, 1935: 1672 Nov 19.
[2] Wren S. *Parentalia. Op cit.*
[3] Sekler E. *Wren and his place in European Architecture.* London: Faber, 1956.
[4] Fürst V. *The Architecture of Sir Christopher Wren.* London: Lund Humphries, 1956.
[5] Wren S. *Parentalia. Op cit:* 319
[6] *Ibid:* 320.

St Paul's Cathedral

In order that the progress of work on St Paul's can be followed over the long years of its building and decoration without undue confusion the discussion which follows is treated under headings which allow a chronology to be observed. These headings are: Old St Paul's Church; Designs and models; Contracts; Finance and accounts; The Exterior; (Progress of work; Structural faults; The Choir; Porticoes and pediments; The Dome); The Interior; (Woodcarving; Metalwork; The Organ; Painting of the Dome).

Old St Paul's Church   When Wren returned from Paris in 1666 it was to the pressing request for a report on Old St Paul's Church. A Commission to repair the ravaged church (*see* pls. 78-79) had been set up by the King in April 1663 and Denham as Surveyor-General, John Webb, and the Master Mason, Edward Marshall had prepared a report. They had called to their assistance several of their most skilled workmen and had agreed that the piers supporting the steeple were decayed and had settled dangerously. Sir Roger Pratt, a gentleman architect of erratic but well learned ability had also given his opinion, and now Wren was asked to report. He started by indicating that he thought most of the proposals aimed at too great a pitch of magnificence, and then detailed all the faults from which the building suffered, attaching reports by the Master Mason and Master Joiner.

With all the reports and second reports before him John Evelyn, as one of the Commission chosen, met Wren, Pratt, May, Chicheley, various ecclesiastics and 'several expert workmen' at the site on 27 August 1663. The 'expert workmen' included Edward Marshall, who had been Master Mason in the Office of Works since the Restoration in 1660, and his son Joshua, who was to succeed his father in retirement in 1677. Their deliberations ranged far and wide and divisions of opinion arose between Wren and Evelyn on the one side, and Pratt and Chicheley on the other. Wren and Evelyn rejected totally certain solutions and determined to build again in the area of the damaged steeple 'with a noble cupola, a forme of Church-building, not as yet known in England, but of wonderful grace . . .'.[1] They offered to bring forward a draft and estimate, which (after much contest) was at last agreed upon and the meeting dispersed.

Within a week they were to have reason to think on a much broader scale for, as previously noted, in early September 1666 the fateful Great Fire of London began. In its fierce flames the stones of Old St Paul's split, molten lead ran down the streets, and the destruction of the church and much else was inevitable. Although Wren presented a detailed report on 'Old St Paul's after the Fire'[2] no one had time to consider it. It was to be another 18 months before it was agreed to clear the site, with care being taken to preserve such parts of the fabric as thought useful. There were other more urgent problems the Fire had caused and they gave Wren and Evelyn the chance to suggest practical methods to bring about a new plan for the City. The craftsmen of the Office of Works were to be much involved, but the arguments and delays were considerable, and the final solution was inevitably a compromise.

Wren's plan (*see* pl. 42) - a baroque conception with radiating streets, piazzas and important buildings set in significant vistas was magnificent, Utopian, and perhaps incapable of realisation. It has been well demonstrated that in any case the City approved Robert Hooke's plan, but that Parliament refused to accept any scheme. The whole matter was then referred to the Commissioners for Rebuilding, of whom Wren was one, but despite his faithful attendance at meetings he had other pressing problems, not least St Paul's, and the destroyed churches in the City. Parliament had decided in 1667 that one shilling should be levied on each ton of coal brought into the port of London, and that the money should be used for rebuilding the City. It was expected that some £150 000 would be raised over ten years by these means but it soon became clear that further levies would be necessary. Three-quarters of the extra duty was to be used for the rebuilding or repairing of the burnt churches, with the stipulation that a quarter of the money might be spent on St Paul's. The remaining quarter was assigned to the City. The Office of Works, for its part, was dividing its time between work on general repairs after the Fire and work on the Palace of Whitehall.

Designs and models By November 1671, Old St Paul's was half-demolished, partly by the use of gunpowder, and the foundations for a new church were dug in 1672-73. There was need for haste for changes of mind had been ever-present. Wren had prepared for Archbishop Sancroft a number of early designs. Interpretation of all designs has led to many varied opinions. The probable alternatives have been assessed elsewhere[3] and the accepted conclusions are summarised here. As the documentation is incomplete and the use of the words 'design' and 'model' do not always imply a two or three-dimensional realisation, there still remains some uncertainty. The earliest design from after the Fire is the one sketched marginally on the two City plans of 1666 (*see* pls. 80-81). One shows a rough keyhole shape; the other shows two rooms, one behind a west portico, with a longer nave and an east rotunda with, presumably, a circular dome. The keyhole shape of the block plan sketched on a variant of the City plan has been likened to the dome of the Pantheon, and also to two designs, an elevation and section in the All Souls College, Oxford collections. The domed space presented so early, but as yet undefined, was certain to give a bold silhouette over the City, and would allow a grand interior setting for ceremonial occasions.

The 'first model' of which a fragment (*see* pl. 83) survives seems to have been a prototype for one or two further models for which payments to the joiner William Cleare are recorded, but which do not survive. One of Cleare's models, for which he received £200. 15s. was shown to the King in November 1672 and was approved by him.[4] As it needed four porters to carry it, it is regrettable that it has not survived, for it must have been almost as large and impressive as the surviving Great Model, and would have indicated an important stage in the creation of Wren's ideas. It was, however, seen by both Robert Hooke and by Sir Roger Pratt. Hooke saw the model some months after it had come back from Whitehall and noted in his diary for 8 February 1673 that Wren had spoken to him about 'the designe of burying vaults under Paules and the addition of a Library body and Porticoes at the west', and that it had been approved by the King.[5]

Pratt, who wanted to rebuild St Paul's himself, voiced objections to Wren's proposal - that it was 'wholly different from that of all the cathedrals of the whole world', all the rest 'being in the form of a Cross'.[6] He cited other objections as to the difficulty of admitting light, the lack of ornament, and to setting the cupola at the west end of the church instead of over the middle. However Wren had in the interim moved forward to a new version, and made preparations for a new model, the surviving 'Great Model'.

Wren's first approach was in the unusual shape of a Greek cross, and a plan and elevation survive. They show a great dome, well realised in the elevation (*see* pl. 84) on a low, polygonal drum. The liturgical objections and the difficulty of reconciling the plan to processional routes led to its abandonment. The final design, and the Great Model which represented it therefore, after many false starts, came into being.

In the summer of 1673 Wren started on this third design, commonly called the 'Great Model Design' after Cleare's surviving model. The King gave formal commission on 12 November 1673 to the several designs Wren submitted, specifying one 'of which we do more especially approve' (*see* pls. 90-92), and commanded the model to be made.[7] The Great Model had, however, already been under construction over the previous six months, due to delay in issue of the King's Commission. The Commission had also appointed Commissioners, and specified sources of money, including £1000 annually from the Privy Purse. The model was to act as 'a perpetual and unchangeable rule and direction for the conduct of the whole Work'.[8]

The Great Model is an imposing construction (*see* pls. 85, 88), large enough to walk inside, and is made of oak to a scale of half an inch to one foot. The Sergeant Painter, Robert Streeter, snr, gilded several parts of it, and cleaned and coloured parts to resemble stone and lead. The inside of the Dome and Lantern was plastered by the Master Plasterer to the Office of Works, John Grove jnr, using lime, sand and animal hair beaten together in the approved fashion. There are payments by Richard Cleare, to 12 joiners for carving, and expenses for the plasterwork and gilding, totalling £505. 6s. 0d. The model was at last starting to represent the architect's grand conceptions for a fitting metropolitan church. The domed circular space was well defined, with the choir, transepts, crossing and west portico entrance divided clearly from it.

Many of the relevant Great Model drawings from the All Souls College, Oxford collection, reproduced here, seem to have been drawn by Edward Woodroffe under the architect's direction. Although the design was assertive in its splendour (*see* pl. 89) there is little reason to assume that it was a signal for the King to knight Wren. The date of that event is imprecise, with some writers assuming it to be in November 1672, and others as late as 1674. Whatever the truth, it gave Wren, at last, the right to stand equal in status to his predecessor, Sir John Denham, (dead some three years), and his present rival, Sir Roger Pratt, who had been knighted in 1668.

The most significant difference between the 'Greek Cross' design and the Great Model Design was the western portico with its eight 30m (100ft) high Corinthian order columns (*see* pls. 73, 94), and the pediment topped by statues, all of which have disappeared. They were noted in 1674 by Hooke and may have been by Gibbons. The sources from which Wren borrowed have been itemised.[9] Principally these were the drum of the dome which resembled the rhythmic conceptions of Donato Bramante, and in the ribbed section above, the ideas of Michelangelo (*see* pls. 86-87). Inigo Jones had put a Corinthian portico without a pediment on to Old St Paul's and this was well remembered by Wren from his early surveys of that edifice, and adapted to the new setting. The dome was arranged over eight arches and may owe much to François Mansart's abortive design for a Bourbon chapel at Saint-Denis which Wren may have seen when in Paris. Finally a design for a Greek cross church by John Webb may have suggested some of the disposition of the Great Model. That all the elements were well and effectively blended, with no trace of arid eclecticism says much for the quality of Wren's perceptive and enquiring thoughts.

It might well be thought by the long process and submission of designs, and notwithstanding that the Great Model scheme had, according to *Parentalia* pleased 'Persons of Distinction, skill'd in Antiquity and Architecture' that work could proceed. The foundations were being dug but still the clergy were displeased. The absence of a Latin cross plan, in which services could be conducted in the choir, and listened to by a large congregation in the nave, was considered a denial of the links with early Christianity and the traditional plan. Also finance was still uncertain, and the Great Model design could not be built and completed in stages when all the work led to the support of one great central dome, to act as roof.

In the mass of evidence which survives about the building of the Cathedral, set out in detail in the 20 volumes of the *Wren Society* (1924-43) (*see* Bibliography) and in cogent summary elsewhere,[10] there is little to detail the negotiations which got rapidly under way at this setback. Wren is said by one 19th century author, citing the 18th century writer Joseph Spence, to have shed tears at the rejection; equally, however, Victorian writers were eager to claim 'that the whole design was given up, probably with advantage'.[11] What Wren did do, for certain, was state that he 'would make no models or publicly expose his drawings' of any further designs.[12] What he had to do, bitter as the effort may have been, was to blend traditional Gothic layouts with those of Renaissance forms.

It was necessary to use the elements of previous schemes. There was need, in the architect's mind at least, to preserve a dome. Several attempts were made to reconcile disparate parts, and it was perhaps to be expected that the design which received royal approval by issue of a warrant on 14 May 1675 - the 'Warrant Design' (*see* pls. 90-92) met with the approval of the clergy. It is possible to detect the weak elements in this design which used the form of a Latin cross, with a choir of three bays and a nave of five. Wren preferred the Great Model scheme with its Greek cross form of four equal arms with an extension to the west.[13] Whatever the reasons for submission of the 'Warrant Design' we must remember that Wren's wife had died, and he was weary of the delaying financial tactics of Parliament. At least the foundation stone could be laid, the Warrant Design was in existence for many of the elements, and the final shape of the dome could be left for a time.

Contracts   After the 'Royal Warrant for the Design Chosen' had been issued in 1675, and the foundation stone laid at the south-east corner of the building, the important contracts with craftsmen (particularly the masons) could be made. On 18 June 1675 'Joshua Marshall of the Parish of St Dunstan's in the West in London, Mason' signed one of the four contracts made that day. Another two were issued for the supply of sand and lime, and a fourth was signed by the mason Thomas Strong. He and Marshall were to do various works preparatory to raising the south side of the Choir. A succession of further agreements with them followed. In all, across the years of building, 1675-1709, 41 contracts were entered into for mason's work, supplies of stone, bricks and bricklayers, carpenters, plumbers, smiths, sand, lime, carving, paving, gilding, and the Great Organ. The details were entered into a Contracts Book and considered by the Commissioners at their regular meetings.

Finance and accounts Apart from agreements, Wren had accepted for himself a salary of £200 a year. The detailed accounts it was necessary to keep were prepared by the Assistant Surveyor, Edward Woodroffe, assisted by John Tillison. They also supervised the daily duties of the workmen, provided materials and utensils, and received money. The accounts show that in dealing with the repairs of Old St Paul's from 1663 to 1674 £14 738. 7s. 1½d had been spent, but from 1 May 1674 to 3 July 1677 alone, the total came to £23 554. 1s. 4½d. The main sources of income and expenditure have been carefully tabulated. Money came from Coal Dues, a levy Parliament had placed in 1667 on coal mining into the Port of London, glove money which Bishops paid at their consecration, subscriptions, loans, legacies, and a general levy or brief on each parish.

The Coal Dues provided Wren with a steady source of income to build, and allowed him to calculate ahead what work could be done in a year. The Dues were also borrowed against at heavy interest rates in the later stages of building. Grinling Gibbons, Jean Tijou, John Oliver and Edward Strong, all leading craftsmen, loaned money at six per cent interest. On 23 March 1697 Wren prepared a full financial statement of future income, and estimated that £212 224 would be forthcoming against which he had to set various debts of £40 969. He then needed to set out for consideration that, if the whole debt were paid, the work would have to be delayed for at least two years. He believed that everyone would be deceived in their expectations, that finance would flag and the various creditors would be uneasy about letting their money lie, even at good rates of interest. Fortunately the craftsmen trusted Wren and by paying some of the interest they were kept satisfied.

Various calculations have been made as to the cost of St Paul's. The statements published by the Wren Society, while meaning little in modern terms, show expenditure of £846 214. 12s. 6d., and income of £878 523. 12s. 3d., leaving a balance in 1723 of £32 308. 19s. 9d. The Coal Dues had provided all but some £68 000 of the total income. The heaviest item in the expenditure was for stone. Over the years from 1675 to 1710 the masons worked over £90 000 worth of stone from various quarries, a third of the total coming from Portland.

Exterior *Progress of work* Before discussing the various parts of the structure a brief idea of progress over the thirty-five years of building may help. After laying the foundations in 1675 the lower parts of the eastern elevation were started, and contracts had been entered into for the foundations of the Dome and those for the north side. By 1678 the Choir was some eight metres (24 ft) above the ground and later in that year preparations for supporting the Dome - its final form still undecided - were undertaken. By 1687 it was proclaimed optimistically in a newsletter 'that a few years will now perfect the Edifice'.[14] It was however to be 1707 before the great west portico was complete.

By the early 1690s Jean Tijou and Grinling Gibbons were providing metal screens and woodcarving for the interior, and Bernard Smith was contracted in 1694 to supply the organ. The final solution for the Dome came about in 1704, and after its erection the competition for its decorative painting was announced in 1707. The negotiations over this were, however, most protracted and it was not until June 1715 that Sir James Thornhill, as the chosen painter, was instructed to begin. The upper storeys of the Cathedral were completed by the addition of a balustrade in 1718 and the arguments over the suitability led Wren to declare that he had never designed or intended a balustrade. By this time he was ready to resign wearily from both the Surveyorship of the Cathedral and to accept silently his dismissal from the post of Surveyor-General to the King's Works on William Benson's appointment.

Progress on the work was given by Wren to the Commissioners at regular intervals, in seven principal reports. Some of the vast problems of controlling progress can be seen in some of the items in the accounts. It was necessary to take up 85 000 cubic yards of old foundation walls and cart away over 20 000 loads of rubbish. In the new Cathedral in three years there had been wrought and set up 37 000 superficial feet of stonework, using 3500 tons of Portland stone, 7500 hundreds of lime, 400 000 bricks, 4400 tons of sand and a great quantity of old sand sifted from the rubbish of Old St Paul's Church.

Structural faults   The grappling with problems and techniques which were not familiar to the craftsmen - the support of the circular Dome for example - led to several mistakes which in turn led to structural faults. Wren's principal masons Marshall and Strong had been trained in the ancient traditions of medieval masonry, and knew little of the new method of constructing the piers for the Dome which Wren was advocating. They were of course experienced craftsmen and St Paul's rose very largely as the result of the skills and labours of the teams of masons which they, and others, led. It may be that the masons had some rudimentary idea of the enormous load which the piers would have to bear - estimated at 33 515 tons, out of a total weight of 44 620 tons - but they were used to the 'elasticity' of older structures.

Wren had decided to use a rubble core in the piers covered with a shell-like casing of Portland stone. There had been vast accumulations of material available for the core in the Old St Paul's, and while some had been sold, the screening and sifting of fine rubbish for use in mortar is a frequent item in the accounts. As early as June 1675 Thomas Strong had agreed in his contract to perform the 'rubblework' of the choir foundations. By about 1680 Wren had realised his great mistake in the use of the rubble core. He then had to undertake the delicate process, through the skill of his masons, of drawing out the facing stone in the worst places in the crypt piers and replacing them with new masonry.

In 1681 he wrote to the Bishop of Oxford in respect of his work on Tom Tower at Christ Church, Oxford, (*see* pl. 63) that he had a great experience in fabrics failing when great caution was not used. He urged that the rubble core foundations at Oxford be taken up, and the methods he had needed to adopt at St Paul's be used. As he does not refer to the matter again, and the master mason in charge was the reliable Christopher Kempster, his advice was presumably taken. At St Paul's the long building period gave time for a satisfactory solution to be adopted for the piers supporting the Dome. In addition Wren devised, and the craftsmen executed, an inner brick dome with a system of chains to lessen the weight and thrusts and bind the whole structure together.

As well as the major fault in the Dome piers some cracks appeared on the stonework on the south side. In 1719 after Wren had retired John James was ordered to insert wedges and to examine the faults again after an interval of six months. There were also quibbles about faults in the designs. John Evelyn complained that columns were placed over pilasters in the apse. It was also said that the Dome had an inadequate diameter and that Wren had lessened it in size because of the faults in its supports.

The Choir By 1678 the Choir was raised eight metres (24ft) above the ground, the greatest part of the foundation of the crossing was made and the Dome was up to the height of the Choir. From east to west it extended 98 metres (320ft) and from north to south 95 metres (310ft). With its apsidal end the Choir was related to the body of the Church by its transepts. John Evelyn recorded the progress of work on the Choir, as well as the complaint noted above. By 1694, the date of his visit, the stonework was finished and the scaffolds, within and without, were being taken down. Its fitting-up with stalls, altar canopy and other fitments occupied the next two years.

Porticoes and pediments In the autumn of 1678 it was agreed that Edward Pierce should build the sections incorporating the south portico of the Cathedral. Finance was coming in slowly but somehow the work continued. By 1680 Pierce had finished his work and the joiners were preparing models for the various architraves, friezes and cornices needed. The trio of master carvers, Pierce, Latham and Strong divided the masonry work around the Choir and its various external faces between them. Pierce was to carve the great cornice within the Choir, and John Thompson began the preparatory work for the west end in February 1686. By March of the following year the west end (*see* pl. 93) was substantially complete for the great portico and (subsequently) the western towers (*see* pls. 108, 109). It was to be 1710 before the great west portico (*see* pl. 73) was completed. Francis Bird was paid £650 for carving the 'History of St Paul's Conversion' in the pediment and the plasterer, Henry Doogood, (a partner to the Master Plasterer to the Office of Works, John Grove), was paid for finishing in the west dome at 2s. 6d. per yard. No contract has been traced for any of the external stonecarving in these areas by Grinling Gibbons. By July 1694 he was being paid for carving in the legs of the Dome, and for the stone festoons under the windows along the length of the nave.

The Dome As early as 1673 Wren had realised the problem of a Dome which to be conspicuous above the houses might look cavernous within. He deduced over the years that there must therefore be two Domes, the outer one to give a bold silhouette and the inner one proportioned to the interior space. There were admittedly great problems in relating the two. In the Great Model design (*see* pl. 89) Wren showed two masonry Domes supporting a masonry lantern. It would not have been easy however to poise the outer one far above the inner one because of the problems of gathering the joint thrust into the system of supporting piers. The final solution came about in 1704 when Wren designed a shallow Dome to complete the interior effect (*see* pl. 96) and then from the same level built up a great cone of brickwork (*see* pl. 118) on top of which he set the masonry lantern (*see* pl. 76) The brickwork was then cased in timber-framing covered with lead. The lantern emerges at the top and no one is aware of the inner supporting brick cone. Several master masons, including Edward Strong, snr and jnr, Thomas Wise jnr, Christopher Kempster, Ephraim Beauchamp and Nathaniel Rawlins (who had been trained by Jasper Latham) assisted in this work.

When Wren had made a full financial statement in March 1697 one of the things he suggested would humour the creditors was to complete the Dome. A great triumphant 'appearance' such as this would plead its own cause and money would surely be forthcoming for completing the whole. His paper was laid before the Committee on 30 March 1697.[15] This Committee which met at regular intervals resolved that the work of the Dome should be carried on as fast as possible, and that a quarter of the available revenue should be applied for paying the workmen. As the method of working was by measure it was in a master's own interests to make his men work with diligence and speed. Writing to the Bishop of Oxford on 25 June 1681 Wren had instanced the current methods used in a building agreement:

> ... there are 3 ways of works: by the Day, by Measure, by Great ...[16]

The first method supposed the direct employment of the builder on time rates, and Wren wrote that by this method he could tell when the workmen were lazy. At the other extreme building 'by Great' meant that the builder agreed to erect for a fixed price. Wren preferred work by measure, according to the prices in the submitted estimate. The work was measured by independent but competent tradesmen 'at 3 or 4 measurements as it arises'.

Wren had already estimated the cost of the Dome and the Cupola. He argued, convincingly, that the decision to push ahead with this area meant all the workmen being engaged. Once begun it had to be carried through to a conclusion, and could not be left long uncovered. We have noted in the section on designs the various changing forms of the Dome's outline. When compared with the design for the Mausoleum to Charles I, made in 1678 (*see* pl. 95), derived seemingly from Bramante's Tempietto (1502) in Rome, the Dome shows similarities.

In 1705 the actual construction began and there are many payments in the accounts during the summer months for erecting scaffolding, fixing templates for the bricklayers, and inserting Jean Tijou's 'Great Iron Chain or Girdle' round the Dome. In March 1706 Tijou received payment of £274. 16s. 8d. for this chain which weighed over 95 cwts. It had been set in place by four masons in nine days in the previous December on the south-west Tower, and further chains by Thomas Robinson were placed in position in February 1707. Richard Jennings was busy centring the Dome. As a master carpenter he was given fifty guineas for 'his Skill, extraordinary Pains, Care & Diligence in the performance of the Centering of the Dome & for Modells of the same'.[17] He had also made three journeys into Kent to choose and mark oak for the building. The cross and ball was set aloft the great Church by Edward Strong and gilded with some of the '10 000 Double Leaf Gold' which was purchased from 1707-09. The pineapples of the western towers were gilded.

At the near completion of over thirty years of patient effort it might have been hoped that disagreement could have been avoided. It had been Wren's intention to cover the outside of the Dome in copper, but the Committee decided otherwise at its meeting on 25 August 1707 - 'It being proposed to cover the Cuppola with Copper, and having fully considered it with all the reasons & allegations for the same. It is the unanimous Opinion of the said Committee that it is better to cover the said with Lead and It is Ordered, that it be covered with Lead accordingly ...'[18] Why the Archbishop of Canterbury, the Deans of St Paul's and St Asaph, Sir John Cooke and Dr Harwood, who were present on this occasion felt they knew better than the architect is impossible to say. They were to adopt a similar attitude on several future occasions, especially when it came to the decisions about painting the interior of the Dome.

The Interior   The richest work in the interior of St Paul's falls into the three categories of wood-and stonecarving, including the organ-cases, the metal grilles and gates, and the paintings on the inside of the Dome.

Wood and stonecarving   By 1696 Grinling Gibbons had moved on to carving in stone and in oak and limewood in the completed Choir, including the case and screen of the great west organ. We have noted that Charles Hopson had prepared certain models for important features of the interior decoration such as choir stalls, organ-cases and other items. Some of Gibbons's carving, skilful as it was, was however giving concern as to its price.

In July 1696 John Oliver, Assistant Surveyor at St Paul's was instructed to compare the measurement Gibbons had set down in his bill with his own specially taken measurement. Gibbons had to put his prices to this measurement as the one he intended to stand by and no money was agreed. In September Wren was instructed to adjust certain of the prices with Gibbons, particularly in respect of certain work on the organ-cases (*see* pl. 131).

Apart from Gibbons the woodcarver of similar importance working at St Paul's was Jonathan Maine of Oxford, whose work at Trinity College, Oxford, Burghley House, Northamptonshire and Kiveton House, Yorkshire had earned him a substantial reputation. Maine seems to have been on friendly terms with the Assistant Surveyor, but his work falls just a little short of the sensitive carving by Gibbons.

Gibbons, as we have noted, started with carving flowers in stone high in the four spandrels beneath the Dome and continued with the festoons beneath the windows. His greatest surviving work however is in the woodcarving in the Choir (*see* pls 122-124, 131), which was originally crowned with a great screen supporting the organ-case. (*see* pl 125). Except for the carved angels on the organ-case there was, in deference to Protestant taste, no interior figure-sculpture. The interior, therefore lacked the full appeal to the senses typical of its baroque counterparts on the Continent. It had all to be left to Gibbons's swirling foliage, doves, pelicans and emblems none of which was allowed to project more than 5 cm (2 in).

The work consisted of providing two banks of choir stalls, a Bishop's throne and stall, a Lord Mayor's stall and the organ-case. The Bishop's throne (*see* pl. 133) has a canopy supported by oak pilasters and two columns, surmounted by four *putti* which bear triumphantly aloft the Bishop's mitre. Such figures also appear over the Bishop's domestic stall, the Lord Mayor's stall and the Dean's stall flanked by the appropriate insignia. While these seats were carved by Gibbons and his assistants the actual construction of them was executed by the Cathedral joiners. The surviving drawings, however, go only part of the way towards the final results, thus suggesting a close collaboration between Wren, Gibbons and the joiners.

The wainscoting in various parts of the Cathedral was done in expensive oak from Germany. This had a straighter grain and was less knotty than English oak. It presented a smooth surface for polishing and was not so tricky to carve. In the execution of the Great Organ-case however Gibbons turned to his favourite softwood. The entire case was carved on all four sides with scrolls, cartouches, coats of arms, festoons and *putti*. Carved frets held the gilded pipes which soared upward in two stages flanked and surmounted by winged *putti* blowing long trumpets, or holding a carved representation of the royal arms. Above this, four more figures appear to support a heavily carved and console-bracketed cornice topped by a metal grille. Unfortunately the whole arrangement of the organ atop its screen (*see* pls. 111,125) was disturbed in the mid-19th century and the organ sides were split, to be crammed opposite each other at the western end of the Choir. (*see* pl. 131).

The woodcarving in the vestries and side chapels was by Jonathan Maine who showed his abilities in the rich carving - still restrained compared to Gibbons - of the Morning Prayer Chapel screen. The accounts from the two artists for woodcarving indicate the work they did; in the case of Gibbons it was to the value of £2992. 11s. 4½d, and for that of Maine it was £1252. 6s. 11d. For stonecarving Gibbons was paid a further £586.

Metalwork Apart from the special work of the French smith, Jean Tijou, the total cost of smiths' work at St Paul's amounted to almost £15 000. Thomas Robinson, who executed the fine gates at New College, Oxford, seems to have worked under Tijou at St Paul's. He provided the iron rails for the Morning Prayer Chapel, the cast windows for the Dome and various chains and girdles used to strengthen the structure. Locks and brass-foundry work were done by John Brewer, and Andrew Niblett was the copper-smith who provided the Cathedral's surmounting ball and cross, and all the brass and copper wire used. The richest metalwork was however by Jean Tijou.

The earliest record of Tijou's work in England concerns work he did for the Office of Works at Hampton Court in 1689 which was to the value of £2160. The great screen for the Fountain Garden, and the balustrades for the King's and Queen's staircases proved his great ability to Wren. Then in 1693 he issued *A new Booke of Drawings*[19] ... which showed a remarkable ability to relate the iron-work within an architectural framework, or one devised exactly to fill a gap, or opening in a screen. On 27 September 1695 he therefore entered into a contract to provide a choir 'Skreen of curious Iron-works' (*see* pls. 120,133) at St Paul's and to finish this by the summer of 1696. He was to be paid at the rate of 40s. a foot in the sums of £100 in hand and

£100 each month as the work required. He was also to provide two smaller screens and infill certain carved wood doors by Gibbons and Maine with metal panels. The Choir Screen is perhaps Tijou's finest work in England and shows restraint (which may indicate the dominance of Wren's ideas) as opposed to the flamboyant *repoussé* work, scrolls and mask faces Tijou introduced in his work at Hampton Court (*see* pls. 34-35).

Paintings Ordinary painting did not form an important part of the work on the Cathedral during the first two-thirds of the time of erection. Windows, bolts, nuts, were all painted as a routine matter but from 1698 to 1710 nearly £2000 was expended on painting the whole interior of the Cathedral. Nine hundred, sixty two and a half yards (881m) of this work were treated as a decorative item and painted to simulate white marble. Gilding was also done around the altar, and the organ pipes were gilded at a cost of £66. 10s. 0d. in 1698. Wren also had all the stonework, including carvings, oiled as a preparation for paintings. When Wren's son, also named Christopher, compiled his collection of notes, documents and reminiscences about the Wren family, short-titled *Parentalia*,[20] he stated that it had been the architect's intention to cover the inside of the Dome with mosaics. The Wren Society editors regard the statement in *Parentalia* 'as a confused recollection' and the section of the Great Model of 1673, (*see* pl. 92) shows a coffered interior to the Dome. The Committee, however, meeting on 3 March 1709 '*Ordered That* the inside of the Dome be painted with figures, but confined to the Scripturall History taken from the Acts of the Apostles, and that such Painters as are willing to undertake the same, do bring their Designs & proposalls (both as to sume & time) to the Commissioners at the Chapter House of the said Church on Tuesday the 5th Day of April next ...'[21]

On 5 April 1709 the Committee met and considered designs submitted by Thornhill, Pellegrini, Catenaro, Brechet and Cheron.[22] Consideration was deferred in the matter until the next meeting. Sir James Thornhill and Pellegrini by the superiority of their designs emerged in the lead after the first round of competition. They were commissioned by the Committee, at its resumed meeting of 11 February 1710 to paint specimens in model cupolas specially made for the purpose. It was perhaps a foregone conclusion that no Romish decorator would be given the task of painting the Dome, and while Wren is said to have preferred Pellegrini's work he was again overruled. He had been ignored on the question of using copper instead of lead for the Dome; now it seemed as if he was to be overruled about the paintings. After protracted negotiation the Committee, meeting on 28 June 1715 ordered that Thornhill should paint the Dome in *basso-relievo* and finish it by the middle of 1716 at a cost of £4000.

On 13 September of the same year Thornhill was paid a first instalment of £200 on account. The following July he was asked to give an estimate for painting and gilding the lantern. This he did but consideration of it was delayed for almost two years. By the middle of 1716 Thornhill, with two or three painters working under him, was ready to start painting the story of St Paul (*see* pls. 113-116). The Commissioners after their tardiness, and possibly pleased with the progress and nature of the work Thornhill was conducting, agreed on 4 March 1718 to have the lantern painted, and by further decisions he also painted a series of monochrome friezes round the Whispering

Gallery. In summary therefore his work was in three phases and totalled £6575.

1715	Cupola	(£4000)
1717	Lantern	(£450)
1718-19	Whispering Gallery	(£2125)

Unfortunately the ruling by the Commissioners that the work should be in monochrome meant that little life and warmth was added by the paintings to Wren's austere interior. While Wren may have felt that the choice of Pellegrini would have provided a great colourful fresco at the crossing, no one in England, other than Thornhill, was capable of even providing what the Commissioners had decided. It finished the Cathedral in an adequate enough way, to their minds at least.

References and notes

[1] Wren S. *Parentalia. Op cit:* 276

[2] Wren's report is printed In: Bolton A T, Hendry H D, eds. *The Wren Society.* London: 1924-43; **XIII:** 20-22.

[3] Fürst V. *Op cit:* 27-30. *See* Bibliography.

[4] *Ibid:* 30-31; 189 fn 201; 190 fn 221 seems to have been the first to notice this second (now missing) model. Three models are noted In: Bolton A T, Hendry H D, eds. *Op cit:* **XVI:** 205-206, and the first and third (Great Model) are illustrated here, *see* pls. 83, 85, 88.

[5] Hooke R. *Diary 1672-80.* Robinson H W, Adams W, eds. London: Taylor & Francis, 1935.

[6] Gunther R T, ed. *The Architecture of Sir Roger Pratt.* Oxford: Clarendon Press, 1928. Reprinted New York: Arno Press, 1979: 213-214.

[7] The Royal Warrant of 12 November 1673 is illustrated In: Bolton A T, Hendry H D, eds. *The Wren Society. Op cit:* I:pl ix, and the text is given by Longman W. *The History of the Three Cathedrals of St Paul.* London: Longman, Green & Co, 1873: 98-99 or In: Wren S. *Parentalia Op cit:* 281.

[8] Bolton A T, Hendry H D, eds. *Op cit;* **XIII:**5; 26-31.

[9] Sekler E. *Op cit. See* Bibliography. Also Whinney M D. *Wren.* London: Thames & Hudson, 1971:89.

[10] Lang J. *Rebuilding St Paul's after the Great Fire of London.* London: Oxford University Press, 1956.

[11] Longman W. *Op cit:* 115. *See* (7) and Bibliography.

[12] Wren S. *Parentalia. Op cit:* 283.

[13] Longman W. Op cit: 110, and Birch G. *London Churches of the 17th and 18th Centuries.* London: Batsford, 1896:15.

[14] The newsletter text of 1 September 1687 is printed In: Bolton A T, Hendry H D, eds. *Op cit;* **XIII:**xviii.

[15] *Ibid;* **XVI:**85.

[16] *Ibid;* **V:**20.

[17] *Ibid;* **XV:**145.

[18] *Ibid;* **XVI:**104-105.

[19] Tijou J. *A new Booke of Drawings containing severall sortes of Iron worke.* Sold by the author in London, 1693.

[20] Wren S. *Parentalia. Op cit.*

[21] Bolton A T, Hendry H D, eds. *Op cit;* **XVI:**107.

[22] Croft-Murray E. *Decorative Painting in England, 1537-1837.* London: Country Life, 1962;**I:**72.

The Royal Palaces

John Evelyn recorded in his diary for 28 October 1664, a conversation with King Charles II when he presented him with copies of his translation of Fréart and his *Sylva*[1] - 'I presented him with both, and then laying it on the Window stoole, he with his owne hands, designed to me the plot for the future building of *Whitehall,* together with the Roomes of State, & other particulars ...'. A mass of 17th century drawings for Whitehall Palace have survived (*see* pls. 22-26) for the notion of its creation had been cherished not only by Charles II but by his father. The drawings, distributed among Worcester College, Oxford, Chatsworth and the British Library are firstly drawn in the hand of John Webb and fall into two groups. They show that in the first scheme the Palace was to be realised in accordance with Inigo Jones's ideas of the 1630s. The second scheme was recast by Webb and moved away from Jonesian ideas. Charles I, however, did not live to build it, and when his son took up the idea, as related by Evelyn, only Jones's Banqueting House (1619-22), a fragment of a greater conception, was in existence. It seems, however, certain that Wren had informed himself of all the early ideas. He had also the continuity of the craftsmen, many of whom had worked for Jones, Denham and himself.

In 1669 Whitehall was the chief Royal Palace, and a sprawling complex of buildings, partly Tudor and partly Stuart in date. Many alterations and amendments were carried out in the 1670s, including painted work by the Sergeant Painter, Robert Streeter, and a new altarpiece in which his painted work was surrounded by joined and carved woodwork by Thomas Kinward, the Master Joiner, and Henry Phillips, the Master Sculptor and Carver in Wood. In the mid-1670s the rooms of the Duchess of Portsmouth, embellished, as Evelyn recorded, 'with ten times the richnesse & glory beyond the *Queenes*'[2] were filled with cabinets, clocks, and silver furniture, which had been sent to the King by Louis XIV. Some of these items still survive at Windsor Castle. It was to be 1685-86 before Wren built a new wing for James II, containing a Gallery, the Queen's apartment (*see* pls. 23-24) and a two-storey Chapel. The work exceeded the estimates by about £22 000, being occasioned by spending more on the Chapel than was intended.

It is sensible to go beyond the chronological order of Wren's achievements to note this work for the Catholic James II. So swift was the building of the Chapel that the King was demanding that it should be in use in a little over 18 months from Wren's estimate of 15 May 1685. This affords some insight of Wren's efficiency in controlling the often tardy Works organisation. Six firms of joiners were used, and many of the ceilings were painted by Antonio Verrio, and gilded by his assistant René Cousin. A staircase, with its well, plastered in rich naturalistic work by John Grove and his partner Henry Doogood, led up to the Banqueting House, with its great cycle of paintings by Rubens relating to the Apotheosis of King James I.

For the Chapel all the usual craftsmen of the Works were engaged. The mason's work was entrusted to Thomas Wise, and the Master Carpenter, Matthew Banks jnr, chose his oak and spruce deals from Jacobsen & Co. The Master Bricklayer, Morris Emmett, had so many labourers at work that his lists extend over one and a half pages in the actual accounts. James Groves came in to assist Banks with the carpentry, and then six teams of joiners were assembled. William Emmett, a very skilled worker in the City churches, and John Gibson rushed to complete the work. William Ireland was busy glazing, and a further skilled joiner, Roger Davis (who was at work at Burghley House and Chatsworth), was also engaged. Charles Atherton, the plumber, the Sergeant Painter, Robert Streeter jnr, (he had succeeded at his father's death in 1679) and John Grove, the Master Plasterer, all hastened their men on tasks which took normally a more leisured pace. When the plain work was done the decorative painters moved in.

The ceilings and walls were to be painted by Verrio for £1250, but by the time he had completed his 'Assumption of the Blessed Virgin according to their tradition' (that is, Roman Catholic tradition), the 'Annunciation' over the Altar, and the many worlds of painted figures on the walls, he received £1700. Wren had to report on the bill, and noted that René Cousin had used 8132 leaves of gold in gilding the ceiling, and a further 3316 leaves on the ceilings of the Queen's Bedchamber, Closet and private chapel.

In the Chapel there were to be two organs by Renatus Harris, a throne, and many enrichments in wood and marble for which Grinling Gibbons, and his fellow-craftsman from Antwerp, Arnold Quellin charged £1800. They were under penalty of £100 if they did not finish by 25 September 1686, having been contracted to do the work only in March. They were to keep 50 men, or as many as were needed, employed at the task. With such a large and talented workforce in the many trades at work, the Chapel was finished on time, although Wren, as the son of a former Anglican Dean of Windsor, and nephew of a Bishop of Ely, had tried to plan the sanctuary on Anglican lines. It had to be altered, however, to suit the Roman Catholic priest.

The first service, a midnight Mass, was held in the Chapel at Christmas, 1686. Evelyn had visited it several times during the time it was building, and his diary description of 29 December when the Chapel was opened 'publiquely for the Popish Service', gives a vivid picture of the rich decoration, and the mysteries of the Roman ritual performed by the missionary Jesuits. He came away 'not believing I should ever have lived to see such things in the K. of England's palace ...'.[3]

Wren's position at this time must have been very difficult: the Queen's Chapel in St James's Palace had been denuded to furnish the new Romish Chapel in Whitehall. He had also to make early alterations to the chapel to make space for more musicians and to erect a new staircase and vestry. Within two years of its opening James II had left England and the last Mass had been said. Apart from certain furnishings (see pls. 26,183) the Chapel perished in the fire of 1698.

When Charles II succeeded in 1660 he soon took interest in his possession of Windsor Castle and spent much of his time there. The antiquity of the buildings, together with it being the burial-place of his father, and the setting for gatherings of the Knights of the Garter - of which Wren's father had been Registrar - appealed to the King. The dramatic site on a hilltop also afforded scenic and picturesque possibilities beyond those of any Royal Palace in England, or in the France of Louis XIV.

Windsor was controlled by a separate office from that under Wren in Whitehall. Most of the work on behalf of the Office of Works was supervised by Hugh May who was appointed Comptroller there in the autumn of 1673. He held the post until his death eleven years later and therefore it was to be 1685 before Wren was involved directly at the King's imposing castle.

Hugh May's direction of the reconstruction of the Upper Ward gave Windsor some of its finest baroque rooms in a grand manner. He was also careful not to disturb unduly the general character of the medieval buildings. In the course of some ten years the King was to spend at least £190 000 on the new works, and under May's direction Antonio Verrio was to paint over 20 ceilings, three staircases, the chapel and the hall. Some of these decorations were swept away in the work Sir Jeffry Wyatville did for George IV in the early 1820s, but are illustrated in the splendid engravings in William Henry Pyne's *Royal Residences* (1819).[4]

By 1678 Verrio and his large band of Roman Catholic assistants had completed 14 ceilings. Most of the Windsor ceilings were coved - that is, they were arched at their junction with the walls - and this allowed the paintings to sweep down towards the walls as an extension of the room space, or open them up by painting a simulated sky. Care was taken to see that in iconographic terms the King was trampling on 'Ignorance' or 'Envy' or having his portrait shown by Mercury to the four quarters of the world. In the State Bedroom France knelt at his feet, and the royal theme, so oft repeated, must have been somewhat oppressive. By this time the woodcarvers had also moved into the State rooms to work under the superintendence of Grinling Gibbons or Henry Phillips.

It appeared in Wren's later examination of Verrio's bills that the Queen had not been above interfering with the chosen designs. Wren wrote that 'For the worke of the Queene's Round Closett at Windsor I made noe Contract, Her Majesty haveing changed the first Designe, that which is now done, wch is fuller of Figures, though £300 is Demanded I hope I doe not under valew it at £250. 0. 0.'[5] This was the Queen's Drawing Room, on the ceiling of which an 'Assembly of the Gods' was painted. In the King Henry VIII Chapel Verrio's work amounted to £1000, a fact Wren noted in the Windsor account books.

Wren's preoccupation with St Paul's did not cause him to neglect his main job as a Surveyor-General. One of his tasks was to build a palace at Winchester for Charles II. When the work at Windsor was at its height, just after 1680, the King started to think about another Palace. One of the drawings, which the Wren Society editors, writing in 1930, thought had perished in the burning of the Bute library at Luton Hoo, came to light in 1951. It was an early design and differed from the Palace as executed. The percipient John Evelyn recorded in his diary on 23 September 1683 that after a fire in the Prince's lodging at Newmarket the King became 'more earnest to render Winchester the seate of his autumnal diversions for the future, designing a palace there, where ye antient Castle stood; infinitely indeede preferable to Newmarket for prospects, air, pleasure, provisions. The surveior has already begun the foundations for a palace, estimated to cost £35 000, and his Majesty is purchasing ground about it to make a parke &c.'[6]

It was intended that the Palace should be composed of a central block with pedimented entrance and dome and cupola, flanked by two forward projecting wings (*see* pls. 20-22). These wings were set back at each side at a further columned and pedimented entrance. An equestrian statue of the King was to stand in the enclosed forecourt. In view of the troubles with foundations that Wren had encountered at St Paul's, of which his masons at Winchester (Edward Strong and Christopher Kempster) would be aware, the contract specified certain precautions. After levelling, the ground had to be made even with hard rubbish well rammed down. Where there was any suspicion of soft earth or hollows, flint-stone was to be rammed in as directed by the Surveyor-General. The various rates were agreed and a supply of Isle of Wight stone - from which the old Winchester Castle had been built - was arranged. The masons were to keep 60 trowellers and setters at work apart from themselves, and the labourers needed to keep them supplied with materials necessary for a steady rate of work.

Similar contracts were made with the London carpenter James Grove for laying floors, with Thomas Wise jnr, and Thomas Gilbert for stone (some from Portland) and with Nicholas Goodwin and Nicholas Rufford for burning 700 000 stock bricks. The Oxford mason, William Byrd, agreed to set up all the stone and mason's work, and a further contract for work elsewhere on the site was made with William Wise and Samuel Fulkes. Byrd was to keep 14 masons and setters and seven sawyers at work, and Wise and Fulkes at least 28 masons and setters, 14 sawyers and labourers. After the bricks had been provided, the Master Bricklayer, Morris Emmett, was to set up the brick structure according to the design and model agreed. Further contracts were made in December 1683 with Kempster and Strong in respect of the courtyard walls.

Early in 1684 the Master Plasterer John Grove visited the site and then returned to enter into agreement, with his partner Henry Doogood, for certain of the work. This was to be done speedily, and as compensation for the journeys and care in seeing to the correct performing of this, they were to receive an extra penny for every yard finished and approved by the Officers of the Works. The absence of signatures to this contract were due probably to the death of Charles II on 6 February 1685, which meant that the shell of the Palace was not completed within the lifetime of the craftsmen involved. Although the roof was built on all but the centre pavilion, it was not considered necessary by the new King, James II, that work should continue at Winchester. It was also a time when anti-Catholic feeling was rising against the King, and many of the most influential men in the country decided to invite William, Prince of Orange to come to England and assume the monarchy.

William landed at Torbay on 5 November 1688 and with his Dutch Guards moved to London and to Whitehall Palace. James II left hurriedly for Rochester and France, but was persuaded to return a few days later by his Catholic supporters only to abandon finally his dreams to settle Popery in Britain and to leave again for France.

Within a few months of William's accession war was declared against France but this did not stop the King ordering Wren to prepare schemes to adapt the old Tudor palace at Hampton Court. The accounts begin in April 1689, and have been printed by the Wren Society. By June the foundations were begun. Some material, to the value of £1188, was removed from the incomplete Winchester Palace. Wren had made his sketches in haste, but even his pencil sketches give a good idea of the grand effect at which he was aiming (see pls. 30-31). A pedimented centre flanked by Corinthian pilasters, or perhaps an alternative design with the ever favourite presence of a dome were in his mind. At this time, on 2 May 1689 William Talman was appointed Comptroller in the King's Works. He and Wren became busy at once. The account of riding-charges for Hampton Court, 1689-91, shows that in two years Wren visited it on 308 days and Talman on 300. 'Nicholas Hawksmoor, Surveyor's Clerk' also accompanied one or other of the officers on 303 occasions.

Work proceeded steadily for a short time only, with the usual Master Craftsmen and their men in attendance. The crisis which preceded the Battle of the Boyne, 1 July 1690 slowed it all, and the accounts for that month include only a payment of £65. 15s. 0d. to William Ireland, Master Glazier to the Works. The King had set out on his famous Irish venture in June 1690 leaving Queen Mary as a Regent. The vanquishing of James II at the Battle of the Boyne caused great public rejoicing, but Wren must have been labouring under difficulties in carrying forward the royal works.

In July 1690 Queen Mary visited Hampton Court and wrote to the King that things went on very slowly there because of the scarcity of both money and Portland stone. Work as we shall note also was going on slowly at Kensington Palace, and at both houses there occurred a disastrous building failure. At Hampton Court part of the great trusses for the roof on the Privy Garden front fell carrying away the floor over certain rooms near the Cartoon Gallery. Wren and Talman were called to a meeting on 21 December 1689, and said they would give written reports. When both officers were questioned on their reports on 13 January 1690. Talman tried to use the opportunity to belittle the Surveyor. Where it was attested that piers showed only slight hairline cracks Talman attested that they were sufficient to put in a finger. He went on to claim that the piers were hollow and cramped with iron to keep them together.

The altercations between the two men grew more severe with Talman suggesting one solution, and an angry Wren countering with another. As a compromise the Lords of the Treasury nominated three witnesses to report. At a meeting held three days previously however, the King, upon hearing Wren's evidence, ordered the works at Hampton Court to proceed, unless his officers found material cause why this would be dangerous or ill-advised. No such cause was found.

As Hampton Court progressed, Queen Mary, who had a passion for building, decorating, gardens and arrangements of porcelain and flowers, asked Wren to complete Charles II's Fountain Garden. But at her much mourned death in December 1694 the King lost interest and Bishop Burnet recorded that the King's spirits sank so low that it was feared he too would die. In sharp contrast the Officers of the Works, heavy-hearted though they might have been at the loss of a Queen interested in their affairs, had to do one of their ever-present humdrum jobs. This time it had little precedent. They repaired the stairs at Kensington Palace broken when 'carrying ye Q's body down'.

About Christmas 1693 Wren had estimated that it would take £35 315 to complete the new quadrangle at Hampton Court. By 1697 when by the Treaty of Ryswick England found herself no longer at war with France, William, his chief occupation gone, reassumed his interest is making improvements to his gardens and house. Wren sent the King a letter on 28 April 1699 giving a revised cost for finishing part of the house. He supposed that the King would finish the rooms as decently as their size and position required. In September, Talman also wrote to the King in the belief that he would wish to hear how the work had progressed - that five rooms were almost finished and the great stone staircase was complete.[7] With this insistence from his officers the King allowed the work to press ahead. The building programme appears also to have coincided with the King's desire for a small Trianon close to Hampton Court.

For this scheme Talman drew up a set of designs and the section through the hall depicts an interior which had points of resemblance to King William's palace at Het Loo designed by Daniel Marot. This Dutch artist was in England from about 1689 to 1695, and may have designed the Delft vases in the Queen's Gallery at Hampton Court. The stairs which Talman referred to in his letter had a fine metal balustrade provided by Jean Tijou and the walls were painted by Verrio. This was the King's Staircase (see pl. 36), and Verrio, returning reluctantly to work for the Protestant King, painted in a medley of gods, goddesses and heroes of ancient Rome (see pls. 37-38). The allegory was complicated, 'associating the emperor Julian the Apostate and his satire upon the Caesars with William III as the upholder of Protestantism and freedom'.

The staircase led through to the guard room, and to the five south-facing state rooms. In them was set up a great variety of woodcarving by Grinling Gibbons, and his designs included many for chimneypieces, with woodcarving as an important feature. In the Chapel, Wren designed the reredos which Gibbons carved in superb fashion; it was flanked by two groups of Corinthian columns. Gibbons's work was entered at £941. 14s. 9d. in 1699. Tijou, presumably for his work on the King's Staircase received £265. On 7 May 1700 the Officers of the Works - in pursuance of their regulations of 1663 four of them signed the estimate - made a reckoning of what still needed to be done after the busy year of 1699. They had before them account books which indicated charges on the old and new buildings which by this time, at the end of the 17th century, had amounted to £105 000. They calculated the garden expense in 1699-1700 at £4315. 8s. 1¾d., which included the large sums of £2135. 16s. 0½d. to the Bricklayer Richard Stacey and £1315. 6s. 7d. to Jean Tijou for his metal screens and balustrades (see pl. 35).

As further decoration John Nost and Richard Osgood provided lead figures under the supervision of the Royal Gardener, Henry Wise, and fine-screened gravel was laid in all the walks at 3s 6d. per yard. The covered tennis court was also repaired and as Wren declared that he was unacquainted with 'Tennis Play' Horatio Moore gave advice about laying out the ground, with a stone floor and a boarded ceiling.

A work which proceeded concurrently with Hampton Court was Kensington Palace (see pls. 40-41). In June 1689 the King bought the Earl of Nottingham's house in Kensington and the work of adding to it began at once. The King did not like living at Whitehall, and work at Hampton Court had only just begun when the building failure occurred on the Privy Garden front. As if this was not enough for the Office of Works to cope with, anxious as it must have been without knowledge of the new King's moods, the additional buildings at Kensington fell down in November 1689. Fortunately for Wren the Queen intervened. She wrote to the King in December saying that she had often gone over to Kensington to hasten on the workmen. She wanted to take up residence quickly and all the pressure on them, she insisted, had brought about the errors in the work, but the hand of God had also intervened. One can imagine that this statement, with which few could argue satisfactorily, endeared her to the hard-pressed Officers of the Works. In February 1690, Evelyn recorded in his diary that he had visited Kensington and that, despite the patching and alterations, it made, with its garden, 'a very sweet villa'. It was to be at Kensington that the Queen died in 1694. The whole history of building was contained in the previous five years, and the main decorations came after William's own death in 1702.

In the Kensington Palace Contracts Book, 1689-95 it was stated that the stairs were to be of elm, and the joists and floors of oak or yellow fir. The oak doorcases were to be seven feet high and the floors in the Queen's rooms were to be prepared with extra care. The carpenters' work was to be done so that the joiners and plasterers would not be hindered in following them. In the King's absence in Ireland the Queen was approving drafts, and Thomas Hues was to set to work on the brickwork. Edward was to deal with the Stable and Guard House construction. It is possible to see the annual expenditure from a separate volume of accounts, 1689-94. The total came to £65 955. 8s. 0d.

The joinery in preparing the wainscoting for rooms at Kensington was done by Henry Lobb and Alexander Fort, and after them all the important carvers came on the site. Nicholas Alcock and William Emmett were old friends of the Works; Gibbons was the Master Carver and Robert Osgood and Gabriel Cibber were competent sculptors. The plasterer Henry Margetts was employed by sub-contract to the Master Plasterer, John Grove, who was busy at Hampton Court. The smiths, including William Partridge (who worked for Wren in London and Cambridge) and Jean Tijou did work to the value of £2594. 4s. 8d. The total contracted work amounted to £44 300. 18s. 0d. from 1689-91, and £36 687. 10s. 7d. from 1691-96. Wren's riding charges show that he attended the building on 384 days. By careful paymaster's work the account was concluded with £1606. 4s. 3¼d. in surplus, and each master craftsman and officer signed in the margins of the payment book for money received. Then work ceased for a time until Queen Anne, at the age of 37 years, came to the throne on 23 April 1702. An added complication to the conduct of the Works rose when, little less than a fortnight after, England declared war against France.

At her accession Queen Anne determined to make less use of St James's Palace. At Kensington the plan was to have a State Reception suite, of which only the Orangery survives. On 17 June 1704 Wren, Vanbrugh, Benjamin Jackson, the Master Mason and Matthew Banks jnr, the Master Carpenter, signed a report which represented an estimate for building a 'Greenhouse' at Kensington to a design approved by the Queen. To be well performed they considered it would be necessary to spend £2599 for a building 51 metres (170ft) long by nine metres (30ft) wide. The analysis of estimated expenditure gave the bricklayer about a quarter of this money (£697. 12s. 0d.) and the carpenter £361. 1s. 0d. Work was started, but it was soon indicated by the Master Bricklayer, Richard Stacey, that, like all master craftsmen employed by the Works, he was in a position to stand so much credit, he had already spent £800 without an advance. Tardily this was forthcoming, but many a lesser man would have been penniless well before its receipt.

The gardens at the Palace also needed specialist attention. John Barrett, a pump maker, and Isaac Thompson, an engine maker, concerned themselves with the fountain mechanism, raising water over certain levels and with some form of irrigation. Within the Orangery, Grinling Gibbons provided limewood swags and drops, for the meagre sum of £7 12s. 6d. Taste was changing and moving more towards the decorative painter. The proportioned alcoves and wainscoting were by Alexander Fort and Charles Hopson. It was at this time that Vanbrugh started the process which eliminated the master mason, Benjamin Jackson, from this commission. For some time Vanbrugh had been troubled at Wren's easy practice of allowing Office of Works tradesmen to accept private contracts, and of their doing work when, with a salary from the Queen, they should have been diligent at seeing she was not being imposed upon by others. We have noted the pressures which led to Jackson being replaced by Thomas Hill, who worked at Kensington, as well as at Hampton Court, Whitehall and other Royal Palaces. One of the other palaces hardly reckoned by Hill, as he was only owed £1.10s. for work there, was that at Greenwich. Hill had, however, been one of the two principal masons there and was therefore a competent man.

The old Tudor Palace at Greenwich had fallen into bad repair during the Commonwealth but King Charles II liked a residence near the river, and the Queen's House there, designed by Inigo Jones, was too small to house the Court. John Webb intended that the Palace should consist of two blocks at each side of an open court running down to the river, and his drawings survive. The elevation shows the intended use of great 12 metres (39ft) high Corinthian columns set at each end, and at the pedimented centre, in groups of four. This 'tied' the whole facade together and the remainder of the surface was covered with regularly spaced rustication. The general design of the end pavilions with the great columns bore a resemblance to Palladio's Palazzo Valmarana. This had appeared in 1570 in that architect's *I Quattro Libri*,[8] a work which Webb and his master Inigo Jones knew well, and the windows were a modification of those at the Palazzo Thiene, or possibly derived from Serlio.

Greenwich was always assured of popularity while London was growing in size and population, and the Officers of the Works were constantly engaged in work there. In 1699, 30 years after the completion of Webb's wing for Charles II, Wren addressed King William on the subject of converting the site and buildings of the Royal Palace for the use of disabled and superannuated seamen. The idea met with Royal approval and a Commission was appointed - some 180 members in all - which conducted its business through a small executive group. John Evelyn was appointed Treasurer, and a sub-committee consisting of Wren as Surveyor, the Secretary of the Admiralty, the Secretary of the Treasury and 'other Citizens' Gentlemen and Sea Officers' concerned themselves with proposals, schemes and models (*see* pls. 46-48) for the fabric. Much of our knowledge of these details comes from a pamphlet written by Hawksmoor in 1728. What is clear is that work had started late in 1694 and that five years elapsed before it was suggested that the Palace should be put to its charitable use.

Before her death in 1694 the Queen had expressed great interest in a renewal of building at Greenwich and opposed the then current idea of pulling down part of the Palace. Her Majesty being utterly determined not to let this happen saw, as the only alternative, that of building. After her death the work went on and between 1696 and 1699 all the foundations were dug. Wren's Great Hall (*see* pl. 68) was begun in August 1698, finished in November 1704, and ready for Sir James Thornhill's 19 years of painting which began in 1708. While Vanbrugh may have been connected with building at Greenwich as early as 1703 he had no official connection with the Hospital, other than as a Director, and by this time it was too late to influence the Wren designs (*see* pl. 48) to any significant degree.

In 1695 the masons' contracts were given to the faithful Edward Strong, and to the Thomas Hill whom Vanbrugh mentions as being frightened of trying to oust Benjamin Jackson as mason at Kensington Palace. Thomas Hues was to do the brick-work and Roger Davis the joinery. Henry Doogood, as John Grove's partner, was to do the plasterwork, which was a method Grove was careful to follow throughout his period as Master Plasterer to the Works. Although he might have benefited indirectly his name was not involved in the contract when he was employed on other Royal work against his salary. Hawksmoor was acting as Clerk of Works, and accounts were to be made up monthly. The abstract of payments, June 1696 to July 1699 has been printed by the Wren Society and shows a total expenditure of £36 219. 8s. 9½d., of which almost a third (£11 133. 5s. 4½d.) was for masons' work. This sum had been raised by gifts from the King, subscriptions and free gifts, levies on seamen and fines on French smugglers. Evelyn had kept his accounts with meticulous care and from 1695 - 1701, money flowed in from these sources to the amount of £74 831. 16s. 11d., and had kept pace with the expenditure.

By the end of 1704 accommodation was available for the first pensioners and the first 42 arrived in March 1705, two months after the official opening. By December 1708 there were 350. One of the Hospital's most interesting parts is the Painted Hall (*see* pls. 68-70) which was started in 1703. Originally intended as the Hospital Refectory, the Upper Hall was to contain tables for officers and the Lower Hall for pensioners. It was then decided to paint the Hall in 1708 and for the next 19 years the Hall was closed to enable this to be done. The work was entrusted to Sir James Thornhill, by then the best known English painter of murals. On 20 May 1708 he attended the Board of Directors' meeting in relation to the painting of the Hall, and it was resolved he should proceed with all speed. He left it to the Board to pay him for the work as they judged he deserved. John James was ordered to get the scaffolding ready as soon as possible. Thornhill was to prime the surfaces himself, or with help of his men. He was also to make any alterations in his design, inserting what he could which related to maritime affairs, until his drawings were approved by the Board. The Lower Hall was the first to be painted, and he chose as his theme for the ceiling 'The Glorification of William and Mary' (*see* pl. 68).

By 23 May 1712 Thornhill had advanced far enough to ask the Board to appoint such persons as they thought fit to inspect his painting in the Great Hall. He also asked for some 'imprest money' to encourage the speedy finishing of the Hall, and £300 was granted to him. By May 1714 he was able to tell his masters that he would be clearing away the scaffolding during the month. He was, however, to wait a long time for any money, and before he was paid Wren had retired, and Vanbrugh had been appointed Surveyor at Greenwich at a salary of £200 a year.

On 27 July 1717 Thornhill presented his statement in which he recounted the prices paid to many previous painters for their work elsewhere. He instanced Rubens at the Banqueting House, Whitehall (£4000), Charles de la Fosse working for Lord Montagu

(£2000), Verrio at Windsor and Hampton Court, Marco Ricci at Bulstrode and Pellegrini in work done for the Duke of Portland and Lord Burlington. He made the mistake of hoping that the Board would allow him as good a price as any of these, especially when he had spent six years at the prime of his life employed on the task. The Board thought the Memorial unsatisfactory as it did not demand any specific sum of money for the work. Thornhill was asked to be definite, but when he demanded £5 for each yard of painted ceiling and £1 a yard for the walls, the Board countered by suggesting £3 and £1 a yard respectively. Wearily, and with much good grace in the circumstances, Thornhill declared himself satisfied and attended a meeting on 21 September 1717 to show his sketches for the Upper Hall.

By this time George I had succeeded Queen Anne and the west wall was therefore devoted to a representation of his family, backed by the Dome of St Paul's. The other walls depict William of Orange landing at Torbay, and George I landing on Hawksmoor's grand steps at Greenwich. Before his career was done Thornhill not only had to struggle further for his money - he received £6685 for the complete work - but also needed to argue with the Office of Works in 1720 and 1723 for the settlement of six small bills. Thornhill finished his work at Greenwich in 1727, four years after Wren's death. The Office in the meantime was ignoring him and giving jobs of decorative painting at Kensington Palace to William Kent, who was establishing the 'new and lighter decorative fashions'.

References and notes

[1] Evelyn J. *Diary. Op cit,* 1664 Oct 28. The editions of *Fréart* and *Sylva* referred to were Evelyn's issue of Roland Fréart, Sieur de Chambery, *A parallel of the ancient architecture with the modern ... made English for the benefit of builders by J Evelyn.* London, 1664; and his *Sylva, or a discourse of forest trees, and the proportion of timber.* London, 1664.

[2] *Ibid;* 1675 Sept 10; **IV:** 343.

[3] *Ibid;* 1686 Dec 29.

[4] Pyne W H. *The History of the Royal Residences of Windsor Castle, St James's Palace.* London: A Dry et al, 1817-20; Vols 1-3.

[5] Bolton A T, Hendry H D, eds. *The Wren Society. Op cit;* **XVIII**:148.

[6] Evelyn J. *Op cit,* 1683 Sept 23.

[7] Harris J. The Hampton Court Trianon Designs of William and John Talman. *Journal of the Warburg and Courtauld Institutes* 1960; **XXIII**: 139-149.

[8] Palladio A. *I Quattro Libri dell' Architettura.* Venice: Domenico de' Franceschi, 1570; **II:**17. There are several facsimile editions available, such as the one produced by Dover Publications, New York and London, 1977.

III
'Some Figure in the World'

'... haveing worn out (by God's mercy) a long
life in the Royal Service, and haveing made
some Figure in the World...'

Sir Christopher Wren, 21 April 1718 [1]

This short survey of the work of Sir Christopher Wren has drawn due attention to the established facts that Wren was a competent scientist before he became an architect. That he became the most capable and enduring of architects to practise architecture in England is without doubt. He fell short of genius, whatever that may imply, but through his long-held position as Surveyor-General was able to exert considerable influence. The quality of his mind, with subtle gradations of emphasis, has ensured his architecture a central place in British life. He created St Paul's Cathedral at the centre of the metropolitan capital, and it has survived, with some 19th century amendments apart, largely in the form he intended.

In the early years of the 1660s, after the King's restoration and the foundation of the Royal Society, men of Wren's calibre were certain of attention. Firstly he set his newly directed interest in architecture to a well-organised rebuilding of the churches ravaged in the Great Fire, and, as noted, brought to their execution great skill in utilising awkward and restricted sites. He set out solutions in the geometric forms practised by mathematicians, but invested the shapes with superb control of the space. From early years until the late quiet years resting at Hampton Court he preoccupied himself constantly with work, with exercises on the laws of motion, the circulation of the blood, the weather, the path of comets, the diameter of planets, the testing of all manner of theories by demonstration, and in so doing also refined his artistic sensibilities. The theories in execution were not always successful - the load thrusts in setting up the Dome of St Paul's gave much trouble - but ingenuity of a rare kind based on refinement of medieval precedent allowed him to surmount the occasional mistakes.

During the most important years of architectural work - 1670-85 - we have some knowledge of Wren's life from the diaries kept by John Evelyn and Robert Hooke. While Hooke's record was kept only from 1672 to 1680,[2] it notes an inordinate amount of coffee-drinking by himself and Wren, and also notes them walking together, discussing every sort of scientific and general problem. John Evelyn was also a close friend, but recorded less of Wren's homelife. By 1679 Wren was a widower with three young children from his two marriages, intent on his work and living constantly in London. His office was in part of Whitehall Palace - the 'Old' Scotland

Yard - and he had use also of other apartments, including the lease of the 'Old Court House' at Hampton Court, granted in recognition of renouncing his claim to arrears of salary.

He appears in the bust by Pierce (*see* Frontispiece and pl. 196) of *c* 1673 with a handsome, questing face, and in the portraits by Closterman and Kneller (*see* pls. 136, 200, 202) as small and neat. From the diaries of his friends we know he was a good talker who smoked his pipe a great deal.

In 1681 Wren was appointed to an office he held for two years, President of the Royal Society, of which he had been a founder-member and vice-president since 1674. He attended meetings regularly, served on sub-committees, and also busied his life as one of the Council of the Hudson Bay Company, and as Member of Parliament for Plympton in Devon (1685-87). His High Church background stamped him out as a Tory, and he used his position in 1685 to bring in a Bill, with others, for financing Chelsea Hospital (*see* pls. 56, 58, 71) out of taxes on hackney coaches.

In the auspicious year of 1688 Wren again tried to enter Parliament for Windsor, where he had family connections - he designed the Court House there in the same year (*see* pl. 59) - but his election was declared void. The same thing happened in 1690, but he persisted and was elected for Weymouth in December 1701. He dabbled in land purchase in the Barbican, although as Surveyor-General it was his job to regulate the rebuilding of London. His way of life, including the advantages of such transactions, presupposes a comfortable income. He was able to buy a Warwickshire establishment for his son in 1713 for £19 600, a large sum for the time. Some of his work however he did for nothing, or, as at Chelsea, for modest fees. His fees for the City churches were said to have been large but no certainty attaches to this. His salary as a Surveyor-General when he took office was a little over £382, to which riding charges could be added. Although this was increased in the 1680s, and Windsor was added to Wren's duties on Hugh May's death in February 1684, the hard-pressed Government always needed money. Wren loaned two sums of £1000 and £1700 in 1685 and 1694 respectively, and in 1706 his salary was £341 in arrears. However he could live like a gentleman even if prompt payment was denied him and his staff. It was also denied him at St Paul's from 1697, causing him to petition Parliament in 1711 for the arrears. Some of his money, when he had it, went undoubtedly on forming his large collection of books.

Wren's library, of which the 1748 catalogue has been published[3] and which included eventually all the leading architectural treatises - Vitruvius (in the 1684 edition of Claude Perrault), Alberti (1512), Serlio (1601), and Palladio (1601). He also had many later editions, including Leoni's English edition of Palladio (1715), several French and Italian works by Le Muet, Felibien, Charles d'Avilier, Bellori, Fontana and François Blondel, Evelyn's edition of Fréart, Pozzo's book on the rules of perspective, and many scientific, classical and topographical works. Understandably Wren also used books in Hooke's library and he possessed those by his Royal Society friends - Newton on optics, William Holder on harmony, Hooke's *Micrographia*, Boyle's *Pieces* and *Essays* and Salisbury's *Mathematics*. Finally the new Palladian mood in architecture, taking place within the last eight years of Wren's life, was represented by his purchase of the first volume (1715) of Colen Campbell's *Vitruvius Britannicus.*

Wren's writings and comments on architecture and on his own work are fragmentary and were gathered together by the younger Christopher (*see* pl. 205) in the adulatory *Parentalia* (1750). [4] The 'Tracts on Architecture' ranged from discussing early architecture such as Solomon's Temple, to the use of the orders, columns, systems of vaulting and (in Tract I) views on perspective, models, harmony in objects, and 'natural or geometrical Beauty'. His meeting with Bernini in 1665 made a considerable impression on him, and what he saw in France became a significant influence at Hampton Court, Winchester, Greenwich and elsewhere. His achievement however was not to bind himself to the rule of the orders, which he saw as sometimes 'too strict and pedantick',[5] and needing some modification of proportions. The symbolic associations of Renaissance form he left to the theorists, and even the greatness of his predecessors, such as Bramante, Michelangelo and Palladio led him to dissect carefully what they did, rather than praise them uncritically.

It would seem sensible, in the absence of significant writings, to look for the development of Wren's ideas in the large number of drawings which survive. But many of these were not from his hand, and his signature thereon merely implied approval of an assistant's draft. The Whitehall drawings at All Souls College, Oxford, for example, are some two metres in length, and treated in shallow colour washes. But they are not autograph works and while it is possible to group many drawings as the work of assistants such as Edward Woodroffe and Robert Hooke the subject is, as Sir John Summerson has noted 'another skeleton which needs exorcising - what are and are not Wren drawings?'[6]

However as and when they exist, the drawings indicate Wren's involvement, and his approval of what they represented. This acceptance would seem to apply to a fine drawing, presumably by Grinling Gibbons, for the monument to Queen Mary II (*see* pl. 60) designed for erection in Westminster Abbey. It is doubtful whether the carver would have been allowed 'a freedom of expression which would go contrary to Wren's taste'.[7] The importance of the design required his supervision and approval, and, since it approached the exuberance of continental baroque, is a pointer to Wren's interest in decoration. The woodcarvings of Gibbons, Edward Pierce, and Jonathan Maine, and the gilded ironwork of Jean Tijou at Hampton Court (*see* pl. 35) and St Paul's (*see* pls. 120, 133) provide suffient evidence of Wren's acceptance of embellishment when kept within reasonable bounds.

Of Wren's important associates the two most significant were John Vanbrugh (he was knighted in 1714) and Nicholas Hawksmoor. They came only late to the scene, and were but a little part of the refining process which Wren had undergone, from the somewhat absurd 'Warrant Design' (*see* pls. 90-92), accepted for St Paul's in 1675, to the realisation of the Cathedral's west towers, 1705-08. Hawksmoor was associated with Wren from 1697, when but 18 years old, and served with him until 1723. In his buildings there is considerable concern for geometry in architecture, which derived from one who had become, in Sir Isaac Newton's words, one of the three 'who are beyond comparison with the leading geometers of this age'.[8] Hawksmoor gave to his architecture a High Roman style of which Wren knew little, but it was still Wren who 'changed the mental life of the world'[9] and gave it a great imaginative building. It is necessary to remind ourselves of this achievement in the light of Wren's experience. He had done little except the churches until he had served as Surveyor-General for ten years, and the first chance to try his hand at baroque interiors on the grand scale for Windsor went to Hugh May. Of all the Royal Palaces and public buildings only Greenwich came near to the great French schemes under the patronage of Louis XIV and his finance minister, Fouquet.

Wren had help at Greenwich from John Vanbrugh who had been appointed Comptroller of Her Majesty's Works - and thus his chief colleague - in 1702. He replaced the irate William Talman who had also been ousted by Vanbrugh from the private commission of building Castle Howard for the third Earl of Carlisle. A soldier and dramatist also, Vanbrugh remained loyal to Wren, and when posts were being assessed at the accession of George I Vanbrugh avoided taking the Surveyor's position from his aged master, 'out of tenderness to Sir Chr. Wren'.[10] He regretted this presumably in the mean actions of 1718 which ousted Wren.

Vanbrugh had a 'castle style' which owed little or nothing to Gothic architecture. It was, however, present in abundance in cathedral and church, and Wren used it, or modified it on several occasions. A significant example is the Tom Tower gateway at Christ Church, Oxford (see pl. 63). The series of letters by Wren to John Fell, Bishop of Oxford (set out in the fifth volume of the *Wren Society*),[11] reveal the architect's difficulties in supervising the work from London. Wren was aware, as he wrote to the Bishop, that his design 'ought to be Gothick to agree with the Founders worke'. In its final form the adaptation made a pleasing structure in a city which had a skyline of worthy spires. Wren was aware, as he put it, 'of the superior claimes of order and congruity' and went on to show his tolerance of the Gothic style in work designed by him or done under his supervision at the London churches of St Mary Aldermary (1682 see pls. 168,182), St Alban, Wood Street (1682-85), and in a late form, finished by Hawksmoor, at St Michael, Cornhill (1715-22).

The first three examples show that Wren was constrained by what was already in existence, as he was in later life when he supervised work on the north transept of Westminster Abbey (see pl. 186). But in all his Gothic work, he retained the objectivity of the artist, who knew when his own preferences were out of place. However, he was soon to be bypassed for any opinions touching architecture.

Wren's 49 years as Surveyor-General were busy and often troubled. We have noted the problem of personal antagonism when Talman was displaced as Comptroller by Vanbrugh. The latter remained as Comptroller until his death in 1726, but from about 1716 Wren could be held to be in retirement. John James also took over more responsibilities at this time when Wren was excusing himself from attending meetings of the Board of Works. This improvement in James's status made Nicholas Hawksmoor jealous. Although he had been appointed Secretary to the Board of Works on 25 March 1716, Hawksmoor appears in most of the Works records as the trusted, reliable but often overlooked assistant. Wren had appointed him Clerk of Works at Greenwich in 1689, against the superior claims of James but this time the positions were reversed.

In 1718 Hawksmoor sent a memorandum to the Directors that a fresh warrant should be granted, in which there might be inserted a reversion in his favour of the Surveyorship at Greenwich which Wren had held, but which had gone to Vanbrugh.

He was informed curtly that this was unnecessary, and that no prejudice had been shown in his employment. In 1719 Hawksmoor and James were asked to measure and make up the Greenwich accounts, according to their best 'skill and Judgment'. It was a move to keep them both in check but all eyes were however on the post of Surveyor-General itself. The tussle came when William Benson (1682-1754), a man of slight architectural and Parliamentary experience decided he would like the post. He persuaded the Ministry of George I to appoint him; the strategies he deployed may be traced in the minute books of the Office of Works and the Treasury, and were set out in the history of the Works, 1660-1782, published in 1976 (*see* Bibliography).[12]

The preamble of 26 April 1718 starts with a long statement about the privileges of the Office of Surveyor. The thrust is then clean and precise in giving and granting 'unto our welbeloved William Benson esquire the Office of Surveyour of the Works'. As soon as Benson was in office he appointed his brother Benjamin as Clerk of Works in place of Hawksmoor, and Colen Campbell as Deputy Surveyor and Chief Clerk.

This was political jobbery at its worst, ignoring for a moment the real abilities of Campbell. Fortunately Benson's competence was not equal to the tasks he assumed. It was soon reported that under pretence of saving money 'he got Sr. Chr. Wren turned out and himself put in his place'.[13] What was worse, was that he condemned certain buildings in and adjacent to the House of Lords as unsafe and in danger of collapse. A Committee of the House proved the allegations to be incorrect and the discredited Benson was relieved of his recently acquired post on 17 July 1719. Four months earlier Wren had broken his silence to write, on 21 April, to the Lords of the Treasury. He noted his long service to the Crown and chided the Commissioners at the mismanagement of his office. He indicated grounds for 'censuring former managements' but submitted wearily (in the phrase at the head of this section) that 'haveing worn out (by God's mercy) a long life in the Royal Service' he hoped that he would be allowed to retire, and finally die in peace. He retired to his house at Westminster and the apartment he had at Hampton Court.

The young Christopher Wren wrote in *Parentalia* that in this place:

free from Worldly Affairs, he passed the greatest part of the last following Years of his Life in Contemplation and Studies, and principally in the Consolation of the Holy Scriptures: Cheerful in Solitude ... Though Time had enfeebled his Limbs (which was his chief Ailment), yet it had little influence on the Vigour of his Mind, which continued, with a Vivacity rarely found at that Age ... His great Humanity appeared to the last, in Benevolence and Complacency free from all Moroseness in Behaviour and Aspect.

In his retirement Wren often used to visit St Paul's, sitting unnoticed under the Dome which had been the chief concern of his life. He had outlived his friends, and on 25 February 1723, at the age of 91 was found dead in his chair after a midday nap. The next week he was carried to St Paul's with 'Great funeral State and Solemnity' and buried in the crypt under the choir. His grave (*see* pl. 207), near to that of his daughter, Jane (*see* pl. 204) is marked by a plain black slab. His son at a later date set a tablet on the wall, ending in the noblest of Latin epitaphs:

'Lector si monumentum requiris circumspice'
('Reader if you seek a monument, look around you')

References and notes

1 Wren's letter is preserved at the Public Record Office, London, Treasury Board Papers T1/220 *f* 216. Part of the text from it is quoted by Colvin H M *et al. The History of the King's Works, 1660-1782.* London: HMSO, 1978; **V**:60-61.

2 Hooke's Diary was edited only for the years 1672-80 by Robinson and Adams, *Op cit.* Further manuscript portions survive at the Guildhall Library and in the British Library, *cf* Colvin H M. *A Biographical Dictionary of British Architects, 1600-1840.* London: John Murray, 1978: 429.

3 Watkin D J, ed. *Sale Catalogues of Libraries of Eminent Persons.* London: Mansell Publishing/ Information Ltd & Sotheby Parke-Bernet Publications Ltd, 1972: **IV**:1-43. (*see* Bibliography)

4 Wren S. *Parentalia. Op cit.*

5 *Ibid.*

6 Summerson Sir J. Review of Fürst and Sekler (*Op cit*). *The New Statesman and Nation* 1956 June 16: 705.

7 Fürst V. *Op cit:* 142. *See* Bibliography.

8 Newton Sir I. *Principia.* London, 1687; **1**:23.

9 Webb G. Sir Christopher Wren and His Times. *The Listener* 1951 Nov 29:52.

10 *Idem,* ed. *The Complete Works of Sir John Vanbrugh Vols 1-4.* London: Nonsuch Press, 1928; **IV** (The Letters):123.

11 Bolton A T, Hendry H D, eds. *The Wren Society. Op cit;* **V.**

12 Colvin H M *et al. Op cit. See* (1) above and Bibliography.

13 *Ibid:* 58.

Chronology

1632	20 October Christopher was born at East Knoyle, Wiltshire; attended Westminster School to 1646.
1646-49	In London.
c 1649	Entered at Wadham College, Oxford as a Gentleman Commoner.
1651	1 March BA degree.
1653	11 December MA degree.
1653-57	Fellow of All Souls College, Oxford.
1654	Meets John Evelyn for the first time.
1657	Professor of Astronomy, Gresham College, London.
1658	29 May Death of Wren's father.
1661	Savilian Professor of Astronomy at Oxford; received the degree of DCL at both Oxford and Cambridge; Foundation Member of The Royal Society.
1663	Member of the Commission for repairing St Paul's Cathedral.
1663-65	Invited by his uncle, the Bishop of Ely to design the Chapel of Pembroke College, Cambridge. Foundation stone laid 13 May 1663.
1664-69	The Sheldonian Theatre, Oxford, designed after the manner of a Roman theatre, but given a ceiling and roof. Opened 9 July 1669.
1665-66	Went to Paris 'to survey the most esteem'd Fabricks ...'; met the Italian sculptor, Bernini.
1666	Submitted to Charles II a plan for rebuilding London after the Great Fire; October, appointed member of the Commission for the rebuilding of the City.
1668	Reported to Dr Seth Ward, Bishop of Salisbury on the structure of Salisbury Cathedral.
1668-73	Emmanuel College Chapel, Cambridge.
1669	28 March Appointed Surveyor of the King's Works; 7 December Married Faith Coghill, daughter of Sir Thomas and Lady Elizabeth Coghill at the Temple Church, London.
1669-74	The Custom House, London.
1670-71	St Dunstan-in-the-East.
1670-73	St Vedast, Foster Lane.
1670-76	St Mary at Hill, Thames Street.
1670-79	St Edmund King and Martyr.
1670-80	St Mary-le-Bow, Cheapside.
1670-84	St Bride, Fleet Street.
1671-76	St Magnus Martyr, Lower Thames Street.
1671-76	The Monument.
1671-77	St Lawrence, Jewry.
1671-77	St Nicholas, Cole Abbey.
1672-79	St Stephen, Walbrook.
1672	October. Gilbert Wren, Christopher's eldest son born and baptised at (old) St Martin-in-the-Fields. (d. March 1674).
1673	20 November Wren knighted at Whitehall by King Charles II; The Great Model of St Paul's prepared.
1674	Vice-President of The Royal Society.
1675	The Royal Observatory, Greenwich; February, Christopher Wren jnr, born; 21 June, Foundation stone of St Paul's laid (Completed 1710); September, death of Lady Wren.

1676-83	St James, Garlickhythe.	1694-97	St Vedast, Foster Lane, Steeple.
1676-84	Trinity College Library, Cambridge.	1698	Whitehall Palace, rebuilding schemes after fire.
1677	24 February Wren's second marriage to Jane Fitzwilliam, daughter of William, 2nd Baron Fitzwilliam (d. 1643), at the Chapel Royal at Whitehall; November, Jane Wren born, baptised at (old) St Martin-in-the-Fields.	1698-1722	Repairs to Westminster Abbey.
		1701-03	St Bride, Fleet Street, Steeple.
		1703	29 December Jane Wren, Sir Christopher's daughter, died.
		1704	Christ Church, Newgate Street, Steeple.
1677-80	St Anne and St Agnes, Gresham Street.	1705	St Magnus Martyr, London Bridge, Steeple.
1677-83	St Benet, Paul's Wharf.	*c* 1708	St Edmund King and Martyr, Steeple.
1677-84	St Martin, Ludgate.	1709-11	Marlborough House, St James's.
1677-85	St Swithin, Cannon Street.	1710	Christopher Wren jnr, laid the last stone of the lantern above the Dome of St Paul's in the presence of his father and the master-masons.
1677-87	Christ Church, Newgate Street.		
1678-82	St Antholin, Watling Street.		
1679	17 June Wren's 4th child, William, born, baptised at (old) St Martin-in-the-Fields; October, Lady Wren died.	1713	St Michael, Paternoster Royal, Steeple completed.
1680-82	St Clement Danes.	1714-17	St James, Garlickhythe, Steeple.
1680-86	St Anne, Soho.	1717	St Stephen, Walbrook, Steeple.
1681-82	Tom Tower, Christ Church, Oxford.	1718	26 April. Patent as Surveyor of the King's works revoked in favour of William Benson.
1681-83	President of The Royal Society. Appointed 12 January 1681.		
1681-86	St Mary Abchurch.	1723	25 February. Died at his house in St James's Street, and buried near his daughter Jane in the SE crypt of St Paul's, aged 91 years.
1682-84	St James's Piccadilly.		
1682-91	Chelsea Hospital.		
1683-85	Winchester Palace.		
1685	Returned to Parliament for the borough of Plympton S Maurice, Devon. Stood also in 1689 and 1701 for New Windsor.	1738	15 March. William Wren, Sir Christopher's son died.
		1747	Christopher Wren jnr died.
1685-87	Whitehall Palace, Chapel and Privy Gallery.	1750	Publication of *Parentalia or Memoirs of the Family of the Wrens,* completed by Sir Christopher's son, Christopher Wren II and published by Stephen Wren, Sir Christopher's grandson.
1689-1702	Hampton Court.		
1689-1702	Kensington Palace.		
1691-93	Whitehall Palace, apartments for Queen Mary II.		

Notes
on the Plates

The arrangement of the following illustrations is based on the categories used in the standard list of Wren's work given by H M Colvin in his *A Biographical Dictionary of British Architects, 1600-1840* (London, 1978), pp.923-931, *viz* - University Buildings; Royal Palaces; Public Buildings; St Paul's Cathedral - Exterior, Interior; Domestic Architecture; London City Churches; and Memorabilia. Cross references to relevant colour and black and white plates of the same building are given at the end of each note.

All photographs have been provided by Anthony Kersting, FRPS unless otherwise stated.

Abbreviations in frequent use:

ASC, Oxford	All Souls College, Oxford
Colvin. *King's Works.* 1976	Colvin H M, ed. *A History of the King's Works 1660-1782.* London: HMSO, 1978: **V.**
Fürst. 1956	Fürst V. *The Architecture of Sir Christopher Wren.* London: Lund Humphries, 1956.
Inscr:	inscribed
Sekler. 1956.	Sekler E. *Wren and his place in European Architecture.* London: Faber, 1956.
s & d	signed and dated
Whinney. *Wren.* 1971	Whinney M D. *Wren.* London: Thames & Hudson, 1971.
Willis and Clark	Willis R, Clark J W. *Architectural History of the University of Cambridge.* Cambridge, 1896: Vols 1-3.
Wren Soc.	Bolton A T, Hendry H D, eds. *The Wren Society.* London: 1924-43: Vols 1-20.

Notes
on the Plates

University Buildings

1 PEMBROKE COLLEGE, Cambridge, The Chapel, 1663-65.
Gifted to the University by Bishop Matthew Wren, the chapel was designed as a simple rectangle, and was consecrated on 21 September 1665. The front to the street, with four giant Corinthian pilasters under the pediment, is based on a design of a Roman temple by Serlio.
Lit: *Wren Soc.* **V:** 27-29.

2 PEMBROKE COLLEGE, Cambridge, The Chapel, interior looking east, 1663-65.
With its rich plastered ceiling by Henry Doogood (*fl.* 1663-1707), the partner of the Master Plasterer John Grove II, and woodwork by Cornelius Austen this interior resembles a small city church, in many of which Doogood and Grove also worked. The chancel by Gilbert Scott was added in 1880.
Lit: Willis and Clark. **I:** 147; Pevsner N B *Cambridgeshire,* Harmondsworth: Penguin Books, 1954: 27.

3 PEMBROKE COLLEGE, Cambridge, Model of the Chapel *c* 1663. *Master and Fellows of Pembroke College, Cambridge.* (Photograph: Courtauld Institute of Fine Art).
The wooden model agrees closely with the chapel as it was built, except for the circular window over the north door. Its crude finish implies it was made to guide the builder, rather than to impress the client.
Lit: Mimms E H, Webb M E. In: Dircks R, ed. *Sir Christopher Wren 1632-1723.* London: RIBA,

1923: 229-232; *The Architect's Vision* 1965;**1:** exhibition of models, Nottingham University.

4 THE SHELDONIAN THEATRE, Oxford, 1664-69.
The engraving from David Loggan's *Oxonia Illustrata,* (1675) north aspect, shows the original dormer windows, and cupola (rebuilt 1838), also the Arundel and Selden Marbles on the enclosing walls. (Photograph: Birmingham Reference Library).

5 THE SHELDONIAN THEATRE, Oxford. The south elevation, 1664-69.
In April 1663 Wren showed a model of the theatre to members of the Royal Society. The foundation stone was laid in June 1664 in the presence of the donor, Bishop Gilbert Sheldon, formerly Warden of All Souls College. John Evelyn records that the first University ceremony was held in it in 1669. This elevation is based again on a plate in Serlio for a Venetian portico, and on the facades of Palladio's Venetian churches.
Lit: Colvin H M, *The Sheldonian Theatre and the Divinity School.* Oxford: OUP, 1974: 2nd edn.

6 THEATRE OF MARCELLUS, Rome. Plan, from S Serlio *Tutte l'opere d'architettura et prospetiva* (1584).
Wren turned to an antique pattern, as set out in Serlio's *Works,* and planned the Oxford theatre on the lines of the Roman Theatre of Marcellus. The spectators would sit in a semi-circle and the ceremonies took place on the stage at the base.

7-8 THE SHELDONIAN THEATRE, Oxford. Plan and timber trusses engraved in Robert Plot, *Natural History of Oxfordshire* (1677) *f*.p. 274. Society of Antiquaries, London (Photograph: Society).

The building was 20 metres (70ft) wide and of a span too great for single timbers. Wren designed the trusses on a triangulation system, dovetailing the timbers together. He used the ideas of his former Professor of Geometry, Dr John Wallis, and modified his 'Geometrical Flat Floor' to this new use.

9 THE SHELDONIAN THEATRE, Oxford. Engraving by John Buckler of the interior (1815), *Oxford City Library*. (Photograph: National Monuments Record).

Buckler's view gives some idea of the careful disposition of Wren's interior fittings which have allowed it to continue serving the University's ceremonial functions to the present time.

THE SHELDONIAN THEATRE, *see also* pls. 61-62.

10 EMMANUEL COLLEGE, Cambridge, The Chapel range, 1668-73.

In 1667 Wren sent a wooden model to the College. In the high pedimented centre he again turned to the theme of antique temples. The façade is not however the front of the Chapel, which is set back behind the Master's Gallery. The lower wings on the arcades provide a unifying element with the façade.

Lit: Willis and Clark, **II**: 703-709; *Wren Soc.* **V**: 29-31.

11 EMMANUEL COLLEGE, Cambridge, The Chapel, interior looking east, *c* 1673.

The rich naturalistic plaster ceiling was provided by Wren's Master Plasterer at the Office of Works, John Grove I (d. 1676). The woodwork was by Cornelius Austen, who also worked in the Pembroke College Chapel at Oxford.

Lit: *Wren. Soc.* **V**: 28-29; 37-38; 41-44.

12 SENATE HOUSE, Cambridge, elevation, 1674. ASC, Oxford I/55 (Photograph: ASC).

About 1674 the University considered building a Senate House which would provide space for similar functions to those carried on at the Sheldonian Theatre at Oxford. Dr Isaac Barrow, Master of Trinity College, (1672-77), and a friend of Wren, advocated the idea, but shortage of funds prevented the ungainly building from being built. Wren based the hall, of basilican type, on Palladio, with detailings from Serlio, and amendments would have been made in its execution.

Lit: Whinney. *Wren.* 1971: 133-134.

13-14 TRINITY COLLEGE, Cambridge. Library, First scheme, elevation and plan, *c* 1674. ASC, Oxford I/41-42 (Photograph: ASC).

Wren's first Library design, was for an isolated building, square externally, and circular within. It was to have a dome, and the design seems to be based on Palladio's elevation and section for the Villa Rotonda as set out in his *I Quattro Libri dell' Architettura* (1570). It is not known why or when the design was abandoned for that shown in pls. 15-16 below.

15 TRINITY COLLEGE LIBRARY, Cambridge. Longditudinal section and elevation towards river, 1676. ASC, Oxford I/45 (Photograph: ASC.)

This two-storeyed block was designed with its back to the river. Wren sent his drawings and a letter of explanation to Dr Barrow. The front to the Courtyard is open on the lower storey (*see* pl. 17). Between the back wall and the front arcade a row of columns supports the Library floor above. Wren said that it was built 'according to the manner of the ancients, who made double walks (with three rows of pillars, or two rows and a wall) about the forum'.

Lit: Willis and Clark, **II** 533-551; *Wren Soc.* **V**: **32-44.**

16 TRINITY COLLEGE LIBRARY, Cambridge, river front, 1676-84.

With the assistance of his mason, Robert Grumbold, Wren created one of his finest buildings. He made careful use of horizontal and vertical lines. Reference to the section (pl. 15) and the elevation to Nevile's Court (pl. 17) show how the floor was set cleverly below the expected height to allow bookstacks to be set below the round-headed windows. Wren used Ketton stone for the structure, and gave his own services *gratis*.

17 TRINITY COLLEGE LIBRARY, Cambridge, Nevile's Court, 1676-84.

The heads of the openings between the columns are filled in with carved lunettes, and are equal in height to the side loggias. The strong horizontal beneath the windows is deceptive for the floor within (pl. 18) is dropped to the springing of the lower arches - the reason for filling them in. The design allows the Library to blend effectively into the older Courtyard, which was built in the early 17th century, at the instigation of Thomas Nevile, Master, 1593-1615.

18 TRINITY COLLEGE LIBRARY, Cambridge, interior, 1676-92.
Wren took a great deal of trouble over the interior arrangement, furniture and natural lighting of the Library. Many of the tables, bookrests and stools he designed survive, and although marble paving was used for the middle alley, the cells between each bookcase were floored in wood to make less dust. Grinling Gibbons did much fine carving in the early 1690s, under the patronage of Charles Seymour, Duke of Somerset (a Trinity man) and Chancellor of the University from 1689. Several of the marble busts are by Roubiliac. The statue at the far end is of Byron.
Lit: Whinney M D. *Grinling Gibbons in Cambridge,* Cambridge 1948; Green D. *Grinling Gibbons.* London, 1964: 80-83; pls. 110-115.

Royal Palaces

19 WINCHESTER PALACE, Hampshire, elevation of East Court Front, 1682-83, *Winchester City Museum* (Photograph: Museum)
In 1682 Charles II decided that he needed a country house which he could visit 'to hunt for aire and diversions in the Country'. Wren prepared plans and work on foundations was begun in January 1683. All was complete, except for dome and cupolas, when work was stopped in 1685 at the King's death. The plan had been based on Le Vau's plan for Versailles.
Lit: *Wren Soc.* **VIII**: 11-69; Summerson Sir J. *Architecture in Britain, 1530-1830,* London, 1963: 139-140; 4th edn.

20 WINCHESTER PALACE, Hampshire, Elevation, possibly by Nicholas Hawksmoor, across the court front and a side elevation of the main block, *c* 1686, *Winchester City Museum* (Photograph: Museum)
This drawing was discovered by Mr John Harris in 1965 and probably represents a cheaper scheme, under Hawksmoor's supervision, to

finish the Palace after the King's death. The cupolas and roof parapet are omitted, and a low truncated dome was set over the central pavilion.
Lit: Cook A. Wren's Design for Winchester Palace, Hampshire, Colvin H M, Harris J. eds. *The Country Seat: Studies ... presented to Sir John Summerson,* London, 1970; 58-63.

21 WINCHESTER PALACE, Hampshire, Drawing of the Palace 'as Intended to have been finished by Sir Christ. Wren'. *Winchester City Museum* (Photograph: Museum), *c* 1780
This drawing was copied from an original of Wren's by James Cave, and was engraved subsequently, with minor variations, for Revd. John Milner's *The History of Winchester* (1798). It shows the east view of the 'King's House & the Adjoining Offices'. The building was used eventually as a barracks and was destroyed by fire in 1894.

22 WHITEHALL PALACE, Part-elevation towards the River Thames. 1698. ASC, Oxford V/4 (Photograph: ASC)
The whole Palace, except for the Banqueting House, by Inigo Jones (1619-22), was destroyed by fire in January 1698. Wren, working with great speed, surveyed the site, and by March had provided two alternative schemes, with plans and elevations. The Banqueting House is shown in the second design, between the two domed vestibules. The pedimented facades would have stood forward at the end of the wings and would have run towards the river.
Lit: Colvin, *King's Works,* 1976; **V**: 304-13; Whinney. *Wren.* 1971: 180.

23 WHITEHALL PALACE, Drawing of the Queen's new apartments, river front, *c* 1688. ASC, Oxford I/85 (Photograph: ASC)
The warrant to rebuild the Queen's apartments was issued on 16 February 1698, and work began almost at once. This drawing shows two elevations, with the right-hand one in accordance with the river front in the bird's eye view by Leonard Knyff (detail, *see* pl. 24).

24 WHITEHALL PALACE, Detail of Queen's new apartments, river front from engraving by Leonard Knyff, *c* 1695-97. *Westminster City Library* (Photograph: Library)
Compare with the right-hand elevation of pl. 25.

Lit: *Wren Soc.* **VII,** pl. xv; Colvin, *King's Works.* 1976; **V:** 294.

25 WHITEHALL PALACE, Second design, Westminster elevation, 1698. Possibly drawn by William Talman. ASC, Oxford V/11 (Photograph: ASC)

The Wren office worked hard to produce these vast drawings, some over four metres (14ft) long, and showing the elevation from the river. Unfortunately the project was never executed but we see from the drawing how dramatic and monumental it would have been. Indeed it would also have been a valuable statement of Wren's baroque interests and accomplishments. 'There is a greater use of sculptural ornament' (*see* also pl. 27.).

26 WHITEHALL PALACE, Draft plan of the second design, 1698. ASC, Oxford V/10 (Photograph: ASC)

Lit: Downes K. *Christopher Wren,* London 1971: 102-110.

27 WHITEHALL PALACE, Second design, river front, 1698. ASC, Oxford V/12 (Photograph: ASC)

The second design consisted of a plan (pl. 26) that showed this river front as forming the left side, a park front (not illustrated), and the Westminster front (pl. 25) as making the right-hand side.

28 WHITEHALL PALACE, Two carved marble angels formerly in the Palace, now at Burnham-on-Sea Church, Somerset, 1686.

These two angels formed part of the altar for James II's Catholic chapel in Whitehall Palace. They were carved in white marble by Grinling Gibbons and Arnold Quellin. The altarpiece was dismantled after the King left England, and was taken, *c* 1695 to Hampton Court. In 1706 Queen Anne gave it to Westminster Abbey. Soon after 1820 it was moved again and given to the Vicar of Burnham in Somerset, who installed as much of the work as he could. Other statues and reliefs are in the Dean's Yard at Westminster, and at Westminster School.

Lit: Green D. *Grinling Gibbons,* London, 1964: 59-62; Whinney M D. *Sculpture in Britain, 1530-1830,* Harmondsworth, 1964: 55-56; Colvin, *King's Works.* 1976: **V:** 292-293.

29 HAMPTON COURT PALACE, Middlesex, Centre part of the south front, 1689-1702.

The Palace is a superb example of Wren's handling of a combination of brick and stone. The stone is used for quoins and window dressings and the horizontals and verticals are balanced carefully. The combination of round-headed windows on the ground floor, with a rectangular window and a circular window above for the main state apartments, and a square attic window is repeated throughout the building. The centre of this front is given added importance by the applied columns and the pedimented windows, with the circular windows replaced by carving.

Lit: *Wren Soc.* **IV;** Colvin, *King's Works.* 1976; **V:** 285-297.

30 HAMPTON COURT PALACE, Drawing, first design, by Wren for 'The Grand Front', 1689. *Sir John Soane's Museum, London,* (Photograph: Museum)

The drawing for the main elevation on the east-west axis has a centrepiece with eight giant columns, and an unusual dome. There are allusions to work in or near Paris in the general disposition - the east front of the Louvre and the court facade of Versailles.

The inscriptions on the drawing denote the purpose of the rooms such as D, 'The Kings great Stair' (*see* pl. 36). The scheme was modified in execution, but the drawings imply the grandeur which was lost.

Lit: Sekler. 1956: 159-163.

31 HAMPTON COURT PALACE, Drawing, first design, by Wren for the park elevation, 1689, *Sir John Soane's Museum, London* (Photograph: Museum)

This was to be composed of 27 bays, with a central pedimented block supported on columns.

Lit: Fürst. 1956: 75.

32 HAMPTON COURT PALACE, Central part of the east front, 1689-1702.

Wren's new buildings surrounded the Fountain Court, and this park front was given an imposing order of Corinthian pilasters and half-columns surmounted by a pediment. These were erected by February 1691. This front contained the Queen's Apartments.

33 HAMPTON COURT PALACE, Final design for the east front, 1689. *Sir John Soane's Museum, London* (Photograph: Museum)

Wren prepared at least four separate schemes to house the King and Queen at Hampton Court. This design is almost as executed (*see* pl. 32 above).

34 HAMPTON COURT PALACE, Detail of drawing for part of the Fountain Screen by Jean Tijou from his *A New Booke of Drawings ... for Iron Worke,* London, 1693, pl. 20.

35 HAMPTON COURT PALACE, Detail of a panel in the Fountain Screen, wrought iron, by Jean Tijou, *c* 1693.
The Fountain Garden stretched away on the east side of the palace, as a semi-circular *parterre,* following a design provided by Daniel Marot. The eastern curve of the garden was separated from the encircling park by Tijou's railings, gates and 12 panels, of which this is one. The Queen's death delayed their erection, and they were not painted by Thomas Highmore until 1700. Tijou received £2160 for his work.
Lit: Colvin. *King's Works.* 1976; **V**: 173.

36-37 HAMPTON COURT PALACE, The King's Staircase, painted by Antonio Verrio, 1701-02 (Crown Copyright Reserved: Photographs: Department of the Environment (**36**), National Monuments Record (**37**).)
The approach to this impressive King's Stair is made through an Ionic colonnade in Clock Court. The Stair rises round three sides of a rectangular hall. The walls (*see* pl. 37) were painted by Antonio Verrio (1639-1707) and his assistants with a vast classical allegory associating the Emperor Julian the Apostate with the Protestant virtues of King William III. As in Verrio's work in the Heaven Room at Burghley House, Northamptonshire, the figures appear in front of a painted colonnade.
Lit: Croft-Murray E. *Decorative Painting in England, 1537-1837.* London, 1962: **I**: 59; 237; Colvin, *King's Works.* 1976 **V**: 169.

38 HAMPTON COURT PALACE, The King's Bedroom, Ceiling, 1701 (Crown Copyright Reserved: Photograph: National Monuments Record)
The ceiling was painted by Verrio with the story of Diana and Endymion, above a gilt scrollwork cove containing small octagonal compartments painted with further incidents from the story of Diana. Verrio was paid £400 for this ceiling.

39 HAMPTON COURT PALACE, The King's Bedroom, *c* 1700 (Crown Copyright Reserved: Photograph: Department of the Environment). As well as Verrio's painted cove and ceiling (*see* pl. 38), the room contained wood carvings by Grinling Gibbons, above a marble chimneypiece by John Nost.

HAMPTON COURT PALACE, *see also* pls. 64-66.

40 KENSINGTON PALACE, London, Engraving of the house and gardens by Henry Overton, *c* 1720, *Bodleian Library,* Gough Collection 20, 96/1 (Photograph: National Monuments Record).
In 1689 the King and Queen needed a residence closer to London than Hampton Court. They purchased Nottingham House for £14 000 and set Wren to enlarge it over the next several years, both before and after the Queen's death in 1694. The projecting eleven-bay block (*see* pl. 41), housing the King's Gallery, was supervised in its execution by Wren. Hawksmoor was the Clerk of Works. It was complete by the spring of 1696 when John Evelyn visited the galleries.
Lit: *Wren Soc.* **VII**: 138-139; Colvin. *King's Works.* 1976 **V**: 190.

41 KENSINGTON PALACE, London, The south front, 1695-96.
The King's Gallery, with its four 'great fflowerpots (*sic*) of Portland Stone richly carved', for which Caius Gabriel Cibber was paid £187. 10s., established, externally, the status of Kensington House. It allowed the King to furnish it, 'with all the best Pictures of all the Houses' and to put in 'a pretty private Library'.

Public Buildings

42 PLAN FOR THE CITY OF LONDON, 1666. ASC, Oxford I/7 (Photograph: ASC).
Wren produced his plan to rebuild London within a little over a week from the outbreak of the Great Fire on 2 September 1666. He proposed a new city with streets of three different widths, and radiating streets running west from a civic centre to St Paul's which was to stand in a piazza. Vistas were considered in the context of what Wren had seen in Paris (such as Henri IV's scheme for the Place de France) and the important schemes of Sixtus V in Rome. But it was a plan which necessitated delay because many of

the buildings needed resiting and re-ordering; it was defeated on the altar of expediency.
Lit: Reddaway T F, *The Rebuilding of London after the Great Fire*. London, 1940: 49-67.

43 THE MONUMENT, London, 1671-77.
Parliament, in commemoration of the awesome Great Fire (from which it failed to take the major rebuilding opportunities) caused a great Doric column to be erected. Known simply as the Monument, Wren was assisted by Dr Robert Hooke in its creation. Many other designs, but none in Wren's hand, exist. He disliked the flaming urn as a finial preferring a statue of Charles II or a great copper ball wreathed in flames. Three hundred and eleven steps form a spiral stairway of ascent.

THE MONUMENT, *see also* pl. 144.

44 THE LONDON CUSTOM HOUSE, 1669-71, Engraved by John Harris the Elder, 1714. *Guildhall Library, London* (Photograph: Library). After the destruction of the first building in the Great Fire the Custom House was rebuilt under Wren's overall supervision, and with Joshua Marshall as Master Mason, on a superb riverside setting. It was finished by 1671. It was expanded in the late 1690s but was damaged badly by fire in 1715. This engraving was made prior to the rebuilding by Thomas Ripley. The Custom House was destroyed by a further fire in 1814.
Lit: Reddaway T F. The London Custom House, 1666-1740. *London Topographical Record* 1958: **XXI**.

45 GREENWICH HOSPITAL, First scheme, perspective drawing, 1694. *Sir John Soane's Museum, London.* (Photograph: Museum).
In 1694, a few months before she died, Queen Mary donated the site at Greenwich for a Naval Hospital as a counterpart to the Army Hospital at Chelsea. Wren's first plan incorporated (right) the King Charles Block (1663-69) by John Webb, but ignored the Queen's House by Inigo Jones. Wren intended putting a matching block to the east (left) side of the large courtyard. In the distance, behind a great pedimented portico was a building intended as the Hall and the Chapel. The blocking out of the Queen's House in the centre distance (*see* pl. 49) was not acceptable, nor was it proposed to make way for

a great garden scheme. The plan was rejected.
Lit: Davies J H V, The Dating of the Buildings of the Royal Hospital at Greenwich. *Archaeological Journal 1956;* **CXII** 126-136.

46 GREENWICH HOSPITAL, First scheme, plan, 1694. *Sir John Soane's Museum, London* (Photograph: Museum).
Compared with the perspective view (*see* pl. 45), the semi-circular colonnade in front of the domed block is dominant.

47 GREENWICH HOSPITAL, Model, 1699, wood. *The National Maritime Museum, Greenwich* (Photograph: Courtauld Institute of Art).
In January 1699 Hawksmoor was paid £15 for 'making the first Moddell of Greenwich Hospital According to the Designes & Directions of Sir Chpr. Wren'. It formed part of a group of three connected models showing the whole site. The model was probably the one taken by Wren to a discussion in 1700 with King William III and the diarist, John Evelyn.
Lit: *The Architect's Vision* 1965: exhibition of models, Nottingham University.

48 GREENWICH HOSPITAL, Drawing of river elevation and Great Hall, 1696. *Sir John Soane's Museum, London* (Photograph: Museum).
After the first scheme, and a 'Warrant Design' (as for St Paul's) (*see* pl. 85), was rejected, the next stage was work done between 1696 and 1702. The Great Hall block, viewed from the river, was set out as two domed structures. The narrower vista between them led through a long series of flanking colonnades to the Queen's House. The detailing of what we possess (*see* pl. 51) varies considerably from the drawings, although the overall plan was now established.

49 GREENWICH HOSPITAL, Engraving, *c* 1700. Inscr: 'The Royal Hospital at Greenwich. Printed & sold by Thomas Millward ...'. *Guildhall Library, London* (Photograph: Library). From the river frontage to the Royal Observatory on its hilltop the grand Greenwich conception is well set out in this engraving. Nineteenth century additions now stretch out from the Queen's House.

50 GREENWICH HOSPITAL, The King William Block, west elevation, 1698-1707.
The King William Court, behind the right-

hand domed building (*see* pl. 49), and containing the Great Hall, was begun in May 1701 and finished in 1704. The authorship of the features shown in this illustration is still uncertain. Wren was in charge, but there are many analogies, in the opinion of Professor Downes, 'with the front of Christ Church, Spitalfields and the north end of Easton Neston' which 'point to Hawksmoor as the author'.

Lit: Downes K. *English Baroque Architecture.* London 1966: 50-51.

51 GREENWICH HOSPITAL, The King William Block, from river terrace, 1698-1704.
With allusion to the towers of St Paul's, and after many variations of plan, the scheme of courts closed by colonnades was decided on. This block houses the Great Hall, but the facing Queen Mary Court, containing the Chapel, was only at foundation level in Wren's lifetime, but was completed by Thomas Ripley in 1735.

GREENWICH HOSPITAL, *see also* pls. 69-71.

52 THE ROYAL OBSERVATORY, Greenwich, *c* 1676. Etching by Francis Place, *The National Maritime Museum, Greenwich* (Photograph: Museum).
The Observatory was built to the King's order in 1675 for the use of the first Astronomer Royal, John Flamsteed. Later in life he noted of Wren that 'He is a very sincere honest man: I find him so, and perhaps the only honest person I have to deal with'.

53 THE ROYAL OBSERVATORY, Greenwich, 1675- (Photograph: The National Maritime Museum, Greenwich).
The Observatory was set on a hill, and built largely of old materials. The central building contains an octagonal room on the first floor. Wren wrote to Bishop John Fell in 1681, when building Tom Tower (*see* pl. 63) 'Wee (*sic*) built indeed an observatory at Greenwich not unlike what your Tower will prove, it was for the Observator's habitation and a little for Pompe'.

54-55 LINCOLN CATHEDRAL, The Library, and a detail (**55**) of its doorway, 1674-75.
The Library was built according to Wren's directions, and to a wooden model by John Thompson. Dean Honywood's arms appear

above the door. Lit: *Wren Soc.* **XVII**: 76-77.

56 CHELSEA, THE ROYAL HOSPITAL, London, 1682-92. Detail of the layout, engraved, 1694, by Johannes Kip.
Chelsea Hospital was founded by Charles II for Army pensioners, and was based in idea on Louis XIV's foundations of the Invalides. The King laid the foundation stone in February 1682, and the whole building was roofed within three years. Further work to enlarge it went on, but no drawings of this major building survive. The blocks are arranged around three sides of a court, with the fourth side open to the river. Lit: *Wren Soc.* **XIX**: 61-86; Dean C G T. *The Royal Hospital, Chelsea.* London, 1950.

57 CHELSEA HOSPITAL, Figure Court, North Portico, 1682-89.
Wren provided an imposing porticoed centre block housing the hall and chapel, with wings to east and west housing the wards and lodgings set around a 70 metre (230ft) courtyard. He used brick, dressed with stone (*see* pl. 71), and designed the loggia, bearing a long Latin legend and the date MDCXCII, (1692), to face southwest so that the pensioners could enjoy the sun.

58 CHELSEA HOSPITAL, East wing, 1689-92.
The central part of the east wing with an early use of the giant order gives a crowded effect to the windows and 'betrays a certain visual insensitivity which appears infrequently but in consequence all the more clearly in Wren's (and later in Hawksmoor's) work'. The statue of Charles II in Roman dress is by Grinling Gibbons.

CHELSEA HOSPITAL, *see also* pl. 71.

59 WINDSOR, Berkshire, The Court House, 1688.
Wren supervised the completion for the Corporation when its builder, Sir Thomas Fitch, a leading City bricklayer, died in 1688. The statue in the round-headed niche is of Prince George of Denmark, and was presented to the borough in 1713, by Christopher Wren jnr, who had been elected its Member of Parliament.

60 QUEEN MARY II, Design by Grinling Gibbons (?) for her Monument, 1695. ASC, Oxford I/5 (Photograph: ASC).
Queen Mary's funeral in 1694 was one of the

most elaborate to which the Office of Works, under Wren's supervision, attended. The body was carried to Westminster Abbey on a 'chariot' designed by Wren. This spirited baroque drawing, for a monument not executed, has many Berniniesque elements in it.
Lit: Fürst. 1956: 143-144.

61 THE SHELDONIAN THEATRE, Oxford, 1664-69.
The stone of this impressive building came from at least four Oxfordshire sources, but principally from 'our own quarry' at Shotover, being known as Headington freestone. It had sadly decayed but was renewed as part of the extensive restoration supervised by W Godfrey Allen, 1959-60.
Lit: Arkell W J. *Oxford Stone*. London, 1947: 49; 63; 69; 72-73.

62 THE SHELDONIAN THEATRE, Oxford. Interior, 1664-69.
The Sergeant-Painter, Robert Streeter I (1624 - 79) painted the ceiling on the Theatre's interior as if a canvas awning had been furled open to the sky. His subject 'Truth descending on the Arts and Sciences, and Envy, Rapine and Ignorance overcome by Minerva, Hercules and Mercury' was intended to be complementary to the ceremonial nature of the building.

THE SHELDONIAN THEATRE, *see also* pls. 4-9.

63 TOM TOWER, Christ Church, Oxford, Upper part by Wren, begun 1681.
The two lower storeys with the flanking turrets are of early 16th century date. Wren agreed with the Dean of Christ Church to complete the tower and resolved to do so in the Gothic style of the earlier parts.
Lit: *Wren Soc.* **V**: 17-23; Caröe W D. *Tom Tower, Christ Church, Oxford*. Oxford, 1923.

64 HAMPTON COURT PALACE, The east front, 1689-1702.
The blend of brick and stone was accomplished in masterly style (*see* pl. 32 for detail of central part). The carving in the pediment by Caius Gabriel Cibber picks up the theme of William III's supremacy over the French as 'Hercules triumphing over Envy' (*see also* pl.32).

65 HAMPTON COURT PALACE, The south front, 1689-1702.
As well as blending brick and stone the variety of windows was well controlled to give a powerful effect; in lesser hands it would have proved too confusing (*see* pl. 29 for detail of central part).

66 HAMPTON COURT PALACE, The Fountain Courtyard, 1689-1702.
Some critics feel Wren's elevations to be a little fussy, with the pedimented first floor windows, and the carved stone circlets replacing the circular windows on the outside elevations (*see* pls. 29, 32). The carved decorations however were a compliment to William III for, simulating a lion's skin, 'he could be regarded as Hercules overthrowing the might of France'.

HAMPTON COURT PALACE, *see also* pls. 29-33.

67 GREENWICH HOSPITAL, from the River Thames, 1698-1707.
The four groups of buildings are (left to right) the edge of the Queen Anne Block, the domed Queen Mary Block, the domed King William Block, and the edge of the older King Charles Block (by John Webb). In the centre distance is the Queen's House by Inigo Jones, begun for Queen Anne of Denmark, 1616-19, and completed for Queen Henrietta Maria, 1630-35.

68-70 GREENWICH HOSPITAL, The Painted Hall, 1702-17.
The Great Hall was begun in 1698, and by 1704 the dome over the King William Block was finished. The interior painting by Sir James Thornhill, much prolonged, was not completed until 1717. The painted ceiling of this Lower Hall contains a large central oval with William III and Queen Mary, attended by various mythological and allegorical figures. The Vestibule ceiling (**69**) was painted by Thornhill in monochrome in 1727 with the Four Winds, surrounding the compass. A detail of the ceiling (**70**) shows a figure representing 'Architecture' pointing to the drawing of the domed building in which the Painted Hall is situated. Thornhill received £6685 for his work in the Lower and Upper Halls, and Vestibule, which were painted in oil on plaster.

GREENWICH HOSPITAL, *see also* pls. 45-51.

71 CHELSEA HOSPITAL, London. Central part of the north front, 1682-89.
This colour illustration shows how the dark brick contrasted with the red brick surrounds to the windows.

CHELSEA HOSPITAL, *see also* pl. 57.

St Paul's Cathedral: Exterior

72 ST PAUL'S CATHEDRAL, London, from the south-east, 1675-1710.
The foundation stone of the Cathedral was laid at this corner on 21 June 1675. The masons Joshua Marshall and Thomas Strong collaborated with Marshall being responsible for the south side of the choir, and Strong blending in the east wall and the apse. They needed to be adaptable as many changes took place in the building as its outer walls rose. The tower and spire of St Augustine, Watling Street, (at right), have been restored and are incorporated in the Cathedral choir school, (*see also* pl. 75).

73 ST PAUL'S CATHEDRAL, The west front, 1690-1708.
While appearing to be majestic, the west front with its two-storey design, coupled columns, and pediment relief of the Conversion of St Paul by Francis Bird is a compromise. He also sculpted a statue of Queen Anne in 1709 for the bottom foreground, but the present statue there is a 'very bad copy'. The front is lifted beyond the merely competent by the west towers and the dome, 1705-08.

74 ST PAUL'S CATHEDRAL, The North West Tower from the roof, 1705-08.
This tower (the left one in pl. 73) is flanked on the far side of the portico by a matching south west one. As late as 1701-03 the west towers were still based on the design of Bramante's Tempietto. A drawing for the west towers, partly in Wren's hand, is dated: 'Feb 25th, 1703/4'. The north west tower was built by Samuel Fulkes, and the south west by William Kempster.

75 ST. PAUL'S CATHEDRAL, South Transept front, 1698-1700.
The flat colonnades of the Warrant Design are replaced by two semi-circular porticoes on the north and south fronts. They seem to be an adaptation of the façade of Santa Maria della Pace

in Rome. The carved lunette within the pediment on the south side was carved by Caius Gabriel Cibber, with a phoenix rising from the ashes. The north pediment, by Gibbons, depicts the Royal Arms (*see also* pl. 72).

76 ST PAUL'S CATHEDRAL, The Dome, seen from the roof of the Nave, 1704-08
The Dome of St Paul's occupied Wren's mind across the forty or so years the Cathedral was being built. Its form changed many times and the final design was not evolved until about 1704. It rises from a circular drum surrounded by a ring of evenly spaced columns; with a niche at every fourth intercolumniation. The lead-covered dome, with vertical ribs, rises up to the stone lantern, ball and cross. It is a work of surpassing beauty, taking elements from Bramante and Michelangelo (*see* pls. 86-87), and by brilliant construction creates a shape of great serenity (*see also* pl. 101)

77 ST PAUL'S CATHEDRAL, Painting of the north-west fronts by Giovanni Antonio Canal, called 'Canaletto' (1697-1768), *c* 1754, oil on canvas, 51 × 61 cm Coll: *Paul Mellon Collection, Yale Center for Studies in British Art* (Photograph: Yale Center).
Canaletto visited England on three occasions, in 1746-50, in 1751-53 and in 1753-54. He enjoyed great success with English collectors who patronised him in this country, as well as through the English Envoy, Consul Joseph Smith, in Venice. His view of St Paul's evokes an ideal mid-18th century scene.
Lit: Constable W G. *Canaletto*, London, 1976: 2nd edn, revised by J G Links. **II**: 414, pl. 207 (Constable/Links catalogue, No. 422).

London Churches, excluding those built after the Great Fire (*see also* pls. 72-77).

78 OLD ST PAUL'S CHURCH, London. Etching by Wenceslaus Hollar, 1656. *Guildhall Library, London* (Photograph: Library).
The medieval Cathedral, with its Romanesque nave and Gothic choir had been recased by Inigo Jones in the 1630s. He used classical pilasters in place of buttresses, and built a great Corinthian portico at the west end. Wren made far-reaching proposals for its amendment in May 1666, but the Great Fire ravaged it and left it a ruin.

79 OLD ST PAUL'S CHURCH, Ruins, view towards the south-west, *c* 1672 by Thomas Wyck. *Guildhall Library, London* (Photograph: Library).

This interesting post-Fire drawing shows that part of the old Romanesque nave, and Jones's great portico at the west end, though badly damaged, still remained.

80 ST PAUL'S CATHEDRAL, London, Detail from the City of London Plan, 1666. ASC, Oxford I/101 (Photograph: ASC).

This small keyhole shaped drawing, seemingly first noticed by Viktor Fürst, indicates the early ideas Wren had for a western portico, an aisled nave and a large domed central space.
Lit: Fürst. 1956: 30, pl. 153.

81 ST PAUL'S CATHEDRAL Detail from the City of London Plan, 1666. ASC, Oxford 1/7 (Photograph: ASC).

This early sketch shows again the plan of the western portico, leading through a nave to a square space, surmounted by a circular dome. Together with a drawing illustrated in pl. 80, Viktor Fürst regards this sketch as a vision of the future, when it became apparent Old St Paul's could not be saved.
Lit: Fürst. 1956: 27, pl. 33.

82 ST PAUL'S CATHEDRAL, Pre-Fire Design, Section, 1666. ASC, Oxford II/7 (Photograph: ASC).

Wren suggested in his report of May 1666 in regard to Old St Paul's Cathedral that the Nave vault should be replaced by saucer domes 'after a good Roman manner'. and in one of the drawings accompanying the report, illustrated here, went further by suggesting the enlarging of the crossing, and covering it with a high dome. It was a prophetic foretaste of what he accomplished, finally, in the 'new' Cathedral. The Gothic choir of Old St Paul's is at the right, and contrasts with the proposed treatment (left).

83 ST PAUL'S CATHEDRAL, First Model, north side, 1670, Wood. *St Paul's Cathedral Library* (Photograph: Geoffrey Beard).

By 1674 there seems to have been three models in existence. This first one was made by Edward Woodroffe, a second model (1673) which has disappeared, and the Great Model which also survives (*see* pls. 85, 88). Sir Roger Pratt disap-proved of all of them. Viktor Fürst established the existence of the second model.
Lit: Fürst. 1956: 190-191; fns. 214, 221.

84 ST PAUL'S CATHEDRAL, 'Greek Cross Design', elevation, 1673. ASC, Oxford II/22 (Photograph: ASC).

In the many rejections of his early plans Wren prepared this unusual drawing showing a great dome set over a Greek cross and fitting into a 91 metre (300ft) square. The plan (ASC II/21) shows four smaller domes surrounding the central one which was to rest, as in the future designs, on eight piers.
Lit: Fürst. 1956: 33-35.

85 ST PAUL'S CATHEDRAL, London, The Great Model, from the north west, 1673-74. Wood (oak). *St Paul's Cathedral, Crypt* (Photograph: Courtauld Institute of Art).

The third model, generally called the 'Great Model' cost over £500 to make. Twelve joiners, and the carver Richard Cleere cut many flowers, festoons and capitals, John Grove I plastered the interior and the Sergeant Painter, Robert Streeter I, gilded it. It is almost six metres long, and is worthy of the intended church. It was to act as 'a perpetual unchangeable rule and direction for the conduct of the whole work' and was constructed to a scale of 1.25 cm to 30 cm (½ in to 1 ft).
Lit: Wilton-Ely J. The Architectural Model. *Architectural Review* 1967: 27-32.

86 ST PETER'S BASILICA, Rome, Design for the Dome by Donato Bramante (1444-1514), Section and elevation. From Sebastiano Serlio, *Tutte l'opere d'architettura et prospetiva*, 1584. (Photograph: Birmingham Reference Library).

All domes created in the 17th century were based on one of two prototypes - Bramante's un-executed design for St Peter's, Rome, as engraved in 1584 by Serlio, or the dome designed by Michelangelo, and executed by Giacomo della Porta. Bramante's hemisphere is set above a drum with an even ring of columns.

87 ST PETER'S BASILICA, Rome, Design for the Dome by Michelangelo (1475-1564). Engraved by E Du Pérac, 1569 (Photograph: Birmingham Reference Library).

The executed dome with ribs on the exterior gives a vertical emphasis; and the drum is given additional interest by its paired columns.

88 ST PAUL'S CATHEDRAL, London, The Great Model, interior, 1674, Wood (oak). *St Paul's Cathedral, Crypt* (Photograph: Courtauld Institute of Art).
For note *see* pl. 85, above

89 ST PAUL'S CATHEDRAL, The Great Model Design, 1673 Section, engraved by Henry Hulsburgh, *c* 1713 *Society of Antiquaries, London* (Photograph: Society)
Wren's Great Model design was engraved by Schnyvoedt (*Wren Soc.,* **XIV.** pl.iv) with an incorrect inscription which implied it was based on Wren's *first* design. This error was also repeated by Hulsburgh in this view (*Wren Soc.,* **XIV,** pl.ii). and by the editors of 1923 RIBA Memorial Volume. The design still shows the Greek cross form which met with opposition from the clergy, and eventually from the King. The compromise led to the so called 'Warrant Design' (*see* pls. 90-92).

90-92 ST PAUL'S CATHEDRAL, London, 'Warrant Design' west and south elevations and section, 1675. ASC, Oxford **II**/11, 13, 14. (Photographs: ASC).
In a mood of compromise Wren attempted to satisfy King, committees and clerics by the Warrant Design and 'reconcile, as near as possible, the Gothick to a better manner of Architecture'. He used a conventional Latin cross form, with the choir ending in a semi-circular apse. The nave was given five bays, and the square crossing had short transepts, with a pediment, round-headed windows and scroll buttresses. The section (**92**) shows the lower dome open at the top and the centre covered by a semi-circular dome above the drum.
Lit: Whinney. *Wren.* 1971: 93-96.

93 ST PAUL'S CATHEDRAL, Study of the west elevation, 1702. ASC, Oxford II/39 (Photograph: ASC).
In 1702 Wren was still uncertain of the precise nature and construction of the Dome. Two drawings of the west front, of which this is one, were prepared. Also many engravings showing alternatives were issued by Johannes Kip, Simon Gribelin (*see* pl. 94) and William Emmitt. This drawing shows the stepping at the top of the drum, and the western towers which differ from those executed.
Lit: Fürst. 1956: 200; fn. 501; *Wren Soc.* **II**: pl. xvii.

94 ST PAUL'S CATHEDRAL, Detail of west elevation, engraved by Simon Gribelin, 1702. *Sir John Soane's Museum, London* (Photograph: Museum).
The great skill of contemporary draughtsmen is well revealed in the 1702 series of drawings and engravings, but statues, additional clocks and other details are added almost at will.

95 MAUSOLEUM FOR KING CHARLES I, Elevation, 1678. ASC, Oxford II/92 (Photograph: ASC).
The mausoleum was to be set up at Windsor but owes much to Bramante's Tempietto in Rome. The entablature was designed to have 20 standing figures on the parapet. Above the lantern there was to be a figure of Fame. Parliament voted in 1678 to give £70 000 'to erect a Monument for the said Prince of glorious memory', but nothing came of the project. The basic idea was however used again in the first design for Whitehall Palace (*see* pl. 22), and any thoughts on a dome were bound to be useful in the long gestation processes over that intended for St Paul's itself.

96 ST PAUL'S CATHEDRAL, Dome study, *c* 1697. *Guildhall Library, London* (Photograph: Library).
The domes Wren intended at Greenwich were also important to his thinking over the many possibilities for St Paul's. This drawing (one of those transferred to the Guildhall Library from St Paul's Library in 1980) seems to date from about 1697. It shows a strong likeness to that of St Peter's in Rome (*see* pl. 87) although Fürst illustrates a close parallel.
Lit. Fürst. 1956: 108-111; pl. 155.

97-98 ST PAUL'S CATHEDRAL, Working drawing for the peristyle of the Dome, *c* 1703, and as executed. (Photograph: Courtauld Institute of Art (**97**).
The drawing, in brown ink with a grey wash, came to light in 1951 when a large number of drawings from Wren's office were sold from the Bute collection (Sotheby's 23 May 1951, lot 2/5).

99-100 ST PAUL'S CATHEDRAL, Plan of the pavement design, *c* 1703, and (**100**) the same area of the ground plan (*c* 1750). (Photographs: Courtauld Institute of Art (**99**); Guildhall Library, London (**100**).

The plan, in ink and wash is for the south-east quarter of the central space and shows the design for paving. It is one of a series, but this version formed part of the Bute collection (Sotheby's, 23 May, 1951, lot 3/30). The detail of the ground plan is taken from that sold in the mid-18th century by Carrington Bowles at 69 St Paul's Churchyard.
Lit: *Wren Soc.* **XIII**: pls. 29-30.

101 ST PAUL'S CATHEDRAL, Back of Screen Wall showing the buttresses above the aisle roof.
Looking at St Paul's from ground level (*see* pl. 72) the walls rise in one plane to the cornice, and suggest that the whole interior is of one height. The upper part of the wall is however a screen behind which flying buttresses were inserted to support the vault of the choir. The screen walls also helped to 'control and remit thrusts, above all the enormous thrust of the dome'.
Lit: Whinney *Wren.* 1971: 100.

102 ST PAUL'S CATHEDRAL, West Towers, half elevation and a section, *c* 1702. *Guildhall Library, London* (Photograph: Library).
The care with which each detail was worked out is evident here with scribing points A - E in the section showing each part proportionate to the other. This drawing was one of those transferred to the Guildhall Library from St Paul's Library in 1980.

103 ST PAUL'S CATHEDRAL, Engraving by Henry Hulsburgh, 1713. Inscr: 'The Western Prospect of St Paul's Church with the Queen's Statue Erected on the Thanksgiving Day for ye Generall Peace in Ye Year 1713'. *Society of Antiquaries, London.* Coleraine Collection III/51. (Photograph: Society).
Lit: *Wren Soc.* **XIV**: 43.

104-105 ST PAUL'S CATHEDRAL, South elevation (**104**) and west elevation (**105**).
Both these views were taken from high vantage points before the Second World War by Anthony Kersting. Pl. **104** was taken from Bankside Power Station and pl. **105** from the spire of St Bride's Church, Fleet Street. They show the dominance of the Cathedral so well expressed by the early topographers (*see* pl. 147). High commercial buildings are also conspicuously absent.

106 ST PAUL'S CATHEDRAL, North-east elevation.
Seen from St Paul's Churchyard gardens, and high above the stone column topped by the figure of St Paul, the domed building is dominant, and the shortness of the transept apparent.

107 ST PAUL'S CATHEDRAL, Isometric section of the Dome. Detail of drawing by R B Brook-Greaves, in collaboration with W Godfrey Allen, 120 × 90 cm, Architecural Press, 1927. (Photograph: AC Cooper Ltd.)
This fine drawing, reproduced here from the original collotype in the St Paul's Library, shows the construction beneath the lead covering of the outer dome. In particular the position of the brick cone which takes the weight of the lantern should be noted, and the void buttresses behind the screen wall (*see* pl. 101) can be seen at the bottom right. Arthur F E Poley also issued a book of measured drawings of St Paul's in 1927.

108-109 ST PAUL'S CATHEDRAL, The south-west tower from the Golden Gallery, and (**109**) the north-west tower in detail (Photograph: National Monuments Record (**109**)).
The west towers, and the Dome, were the high points of Wren's achievement in both physical and aesthetic terms. The mason William Kempster finished this tower, with its allusions to work by Borromini, in 1705. The tower contains a fine circular stair (*see* pl. 119) leading to the Library (*see* pl. 134), and at its base is the Dean's door with a carved arch and brackets. William Kempster was paid an additional £20 for his 'Extraordinary Diligence and Care used in the said carving and his good performance of the same'.

110 ST PAUL'S CATHEDRAL, Engraving of the interior of the Choir, by Robert Trevitt, 1706. *Guildhall Library, London* (Photograph: Library)
Inscr: 'On a Day of General Thanksgiving, 31 December 1706, for victory at the Battle of Ramillies, Queen Anne and Members of both Houses of Parliament assembled in St Paul's'. The Cathedral almost complete, with the great Organ by Father Schmidt across the choir screen (divided and moved in 1860 to other positions), was a worthy setting for a great State occasion.

111 ST PAUL'S CATHEDRAL, Engraving of interior looking to the Choir *c* 1720. Inscr: 'The Inside of the Cathedral Church of St Paul's, London. Printed and sold by Henry Overton, at the White Horse without Newgate'. *Guildhall Library, London* (Photograph: Library).
This engraving shows clearly the dominant position of the organ, called by Wren 'a box of whistles', set across the entrance to the Choir.

112 ST PAUL'S CATHEDRAL, Engraved Section by Samuel Wale and John Gwynn, 1755. *Guildhall Library, London* (Photograph: Library). The long inscription of this finely detailed engraving indicates that it was dedicated to HRH George, Prince of Wales, the future George III. The three 'domes' can be seen, the outer one covered in lead, the inside one painted by Sir James Thornhill (*see* pls. 113-116), and the brick cone (*see* pls. 117-118), supporting the lantern. The Dome and its supports has an estimated weight of 65 million kilos, and the distance from the paved floor to the cross on top of the lantern measures 111 metres.

St Paul's Cathedral: Interior

113-114 ST PAUL'S CATHEDRAL, Looking up into the inner painted Dome, Painted 1714-17. Sir James Thornhill completed the decoration of St Paul's with eight oil on plaster painted compartments containing scenes from the life of St Paul, for which he received £4000. The lantern was painted with feigned coffering and rosettes at a further cost of £450. His decorations in the Whispering Gallery (which can be seen in pl. 112) have been destroyed. Various preliminary sketches by Thornhill survive at St Paul's, The British Museum and elsewhere.
Lit: Croft-Murray E. *Decorative Painting in England, 1537-1837.* London, 1962; **I:** 271.

115-116 ST PAUL'S CATHEDRAL, Two (of eight) engravings for the painted decoration of the inner dome, *c* 1720. *Guildhall Library, London* (Photographs: Library).
The engravings, based on Thornhill's painted scenes, represent events in the life of St Paul, as recorded in the *Acts of the Apostles.* Engraved either by Simmoneau or by G van du Gucht the whole series made the monochrome paintings known more widely. Pl. **115** (engraved by Simmoneau) represents Paul before Agrippa,

and pl. **116** (engraved by G van du Gucht, and reversed from the painted scene) shows the healing of Publius after the shipwreck. The paintings were restored in 1853, and again in 1935.

117-118 ST PAUL'S CATHEDRAL, The Inner Dome.
Wren took the weight of the lantern on a brick cone set between the outer lead-covered dome, and the inner painted one. Reference to the section (pl. 112) shows its position. The elaborate timber framing is set between the cone and the outer dome. The use of the inner dome with a central hole or 'eye' allowed an aesthetically satisfying shape to be devised to cover the crossing. The lead surface of the outer dome has been attended to on at least seven major occasions since Wren completed the Cathedral.
Lit: Feilden B. Caring for St Paul's. *Royal Institute of British Architects Journal.* 1971 Nov: 490-493.

119 ST PAUL'S CATHEDRAL, Circular staircase, south-west tower. Completed 1705. (Photograph: National Monuments Record).
This staircase, a masterly display of the skill of Wren's stone-mason, William Kempster, is housed in the south-west tower (*see* pl. 108), and leads to the library.

120 ST PAUL'S CATHEDRAL, Wrought-iron gates on the south side of Choir, 1698.
The French Huguenot ironsmith, Jean Tijou, who was to work under Wren at Hampton Court Palace (*see* pl. 35) provided gates on the north and south sides of the sanctuary, flanking the altar. He also provided encircling great chains to stabilise the dome structure, parts of which can still be seen, although stainless steel chains encased in concrete were inserted 1925-31. The gates are rich with acanthus decoration and were regilded recently (*see also* pl. 133, left side).

121 ST PAUL'S CATHEDRAL, Wood Screen at rear of choir stalls, south Choir aisle, 1698.
The choir stalls, and the carved screens which face the . aisles were the work of Grinling Gibbons. They show his great skill in presenting a satisfying whole appearance. There is also excellent carved work at St Paul's by Jonathan Maine of Oxford. The pierced grilles were the work of Jean Tijou, the French ironsmith.

122-124 ST PAUL'S CATHEDRAL, The Choir Stalls, north side, 1696-97.

Grinling Gibbons's best work in oak or lime-wood may be found in the carving of the choir stalls and organ case for Wren's cathedral. Although the destruction of the terminating screen (*see* pl. 125) and the division of the organ has ruined the whole conception it is still 'the most magnificent wood carving in England'.

Pl. **123** shows a detail of the carving. pl. **124** shows the canopied and hooded Lord Mayor's stall, and the richness of the cornice and frieze - the presence of an unchanging cherubic choir. Lit: Green D. *Grinling Gibbons.* London, 1964: 90-94.

125 ST PAUL'S CATHEDRAL, Engraving of the inside of the Choir, *c* 1720, Inscr: 'The Inside of the Choir of ye Cathedral Church of St Paul's, London' (also in Latin), by Bernard Lens and Johannes Kip, *Guildhall Library, London* (Photograph: Library).

Here is the interior Wren devised: the choir stalls at north (*see* pls. 122-124) and south, the screen and organ set against the void of the crossing and Tijou's sanctuary gates (*see* pl. 120).

126-127 ST PAUL'S CATHEDRAL, The Library Gallery, and a detail of plasterwork on the pilasters.

A whole team of plasterers under the direction of Chrysostom Wilkins laboured at the many plain and decorative panels the furnishing of St Paul's demanded. The Library was created about 1704 above the present Chapel of St Michael and St George and is served by the circular staircase (*see* pl. 119).

LIBRARY, *see also,* pls. 134-135.

128 ST PAUL'S CATHEDRAL, The Nave, looking east.

When St Paul's was restored after the Second World War the Victorian glass was removed, and the plain glass (seen in the contemporary engravings, *see* pl. 110) was reinstated. The light rakes over the cream-grey and brownish stone, adorned by gilding. The nave comprises three bays with the great supporting piers of Portland stone defined by Corinthian pilasters. The main entablature above the arches has a gilded iron work balcony. The arches and saucer-domes are edged in darker Ketton stone, but the domes are

constructed of brick plastered over, a lighter form of construction. This pre-war photograph shows the High Altar of 1883 by G F Bodley and T Garner, which was destroyed by a bomb on 10 October 1940.

129 ST PAUL'S CATHEDRAL, The North Transept.

Two of the eight great piers faced with Corinthian pilasters which support the Dome are seen in this view. Due to changes in plan the interval between the piers was unequal, and was solved aesthetically at least, by the insertion of upper and lower elliptical arches, to match the coffered great arches (*see also* pl. 130).

130 ST PAUL'S CATHEDRAL, The Choir and High Altar, from the Crossing.

Although the service could be followed more easily by the removal of the Screen and Organ in 1860 something of what was done can be noted in this view. The organ case is now divided at the north and south sides of the Choir, allowing an uninterrupted vista to the new altar and baldacchino by Stephen Dykes Bower and Godfrey Allen, consecrated in 1958. (*see also* pls. 111 and 131.)

131 ST PAUL'S CATHEDRAL, The Crossing and the Choir.

The careful disposition of space in the central area beneath the Dome and the choir aisles give interesting perspective views to the eye. The Whispering Gallery can be seen beneath the windows in the drum. The present pulpit which replaced the original Wren pulpit was installed in 1964. The original was set on wheels so that it could be moved about. Such a pulpit can be noted in pl. 125.

132 ST PAUL'S CATHEDRAL, The Choir, looking east.

The mid-Victorians disapproved of the Cathedral because it was not Gothic. They did much to amend its decoration, including the insertion of a marble reredos (destroyed in 1940), and the mosaic decoration of the apse. The new altar and baldacchino, built to a Wren model, and consecrated on 8 May 1958, replace the previous High Altar, destroyed by a bomb on 10 October 1940. In the style of Bernini it complements the best of the surviving Wren decoration.

133 ST PAUL'S CATHEDRAL, The Choir Stalls, north side, 1696-97.

The majestic carved oak sweep of Grinling Gibbons's choir stalls on the north and south side of the Choir (*see* pl. 121) can be seen in a further section here. Adjacent to Jean Tijou's wrought iron gate (one of two, *see* pl. 120), Gibbons carved in oak the superb Bishop's throne for Bishop Henry Compton (1632-1713); a riot of flowers and *putti*, with every virtuoso swirl approved by Wren.

Lit: *Wren Soc.* **II**: pls. xxvii, xxix; **III**, pls. xxxiv, xxxv; Green D. *Grinling Gibbons*, London, 1964: 92.

134-135 ST PAUL'S CATHEDRAL, The Library, and a detail (**135**) of a carved wood bracket.

The Library, an austere galleried room was created in a south-west corner of the Cathedral. The underneath of the Gallery has attractive carved wood brackets by Jonathan Maine of Oxford, a competent exercise of acanthus scrolling (*see also* pls. 126-127).

136 SIR CHRISTOPHER WREN, 1632-1723, Portrait, oil on canvas, 124 × 105 cm, *c*1693-95, by John Closterman (1660-1711), *President and Fellows of The Royal Society,* (Photograph: Society).

Closterman came to London from Osnabrück about 1681, and entered into partnership with John Riley. The architect is shown with St Paul's in the background. The Dome and west towers differ from what was executed. The portrait was engraved by E Kirkhall in the 1730s, and presented to The Royal Society in 1750 by Stephen Wren.

Exh: National Portrait Gallery, London, *John Closterman: Master of the English Baroque, Exhibition,* Summer 1981, No. 10

Lit: Robinson N H. *The Royal Society Catalogue of Portraits.* London, 1980: 332.

London City Churches

137 ST VEDAST, Foster Lane, 1670-73, rebuilt 1695-1701, tower completed 1709-12.

The old church and tower were patched up after the Great Fire, but in the late 17th century Wren gave designs for a rebuilding. The experienced mason in charge was Edward Strong, who with Joshua Marshall, led the early teams building at St Paul's Cathedral.

The steeple with its concave stage, grouped diagonal pilasters, a convex stage, and an obelisk spire is a complex baroque deviation showing some influence from Borromini. The church was gutted by bombing in 1940, reconstructed by S E Dykes Bower, and reopened in 1963. The furnishing came from other damaged City churches.

138 LONDON, The Thames from the terrace of Somerset House, St Paul's Cathedral in the distance. Painting, oil on canvas, 105 × 186 cm, by Giovanni Antonio Canaletto, *c* 1750-51. *(Reproduced by gracious permission of Her Majesty the Queen.)*

This painting, one of three versions, was done on Canaletto's second English visit, and was acquired by George III from Consul Joseph Smith in the 1760s.

Lit: Constable W G. *Canaletto.* London 1976: 2nd edn. revised by J L Links, **II**: 418; pl. 79, (Constable/Links catalogue, No. 428).

139-140 ST MARY-LE-BOW, Cheapside, from the south-west, 1670-73; steeple completed 1680, and rebuilt 1764, 1818-20, 1956-61; Interior (**140**).

This is probably Wren's best known steeple, on a tower standing out in Cheapside, on the way to St Paul's itself. At the base of the tower the Doric doorways are recessed in niches and the tower is connected to the body of the church by a vestry. 'The base of the spire is a circular Corinthian temple from the balustrade of which rise curved flying buttresses. A smaller temple of columns supports more brackets and the soaring obelisk spire'.

The church itself is modelled on the Basilica of Maxentius at Rome. The interior has a nave and aisles, and three arches on piers with Corinthian columns attached. The nave itself is covered with an elliptical arched ceiling. The church was wrecked in 1941, and after extensive restoration by Laurence King, reconsecrated on 11 June 1964. The interior has been arranged 'on contemporary liturgical lines'. Wren would have disapproved of the stained glass.

ST MARY-LE-BOW, *see also* pls. 153-154

141 ST LAWRENCE, JEWRY, Gresham Street, 1671-77, from the east.

Adjacent to Guildhall this is the church of the Lord Mayor and Corporation of London. King Charles II attended its opening service in 1677.

As the site was open to the east Wren set four half-columns with Corinthian capitals to carry the pediment. With flanking stone swags of fruit and flowers, niches, and pilasters at the corners it gives distinction to the simple, one-aisled rectangle. The church was damaged extensively on 29 December 1940 and rebuilt, 1954-57 to the design of Mr Cecil Brown.

142 ST STEPHEN, Walbrook, 1672-79. The interior, repaired and restored 1830-34, 1951-54. The teams of craftsmen assembled by Wren for the City churches included all the competent names who were to excel in the erection of St Paul's - Edward Strong and Christopher Kempster, John Longland, Jonathan Maine, and John Grove. James Elmes wrote poetically in his *Life* of Wren (1823) of 'a lovely band of Corinthian columns of beauteous proportions appear in magic mazes before you ...' There are 16 of them and they organise the interior space to a point where the simple rectangle disappears, and attention is focussed on the wood and plaster dome supported on eight of the columns. The dome was mostly destroyed in 1941, and reconstructed 1951-52: the church was re-hallowed on 29 March 1954 (*see also* pl. 173).

143 ST MARY ABCHURCH, Abchurch lane, 1681-86. Interior looking east.
The bricklayers John Evans and John Bridges created a dark red brick church in the 1680s. By 1708 it was being 'repaired and beautified' and it seems probable at this time that the dome was painted. The painting - of angels making music and adoring the Hebrew name of God, surrounded by a feigned stone cornice supported by figures of the Christian virtues - has been attributed to Isaac Fuller II, or to William Snow, to whom payments were made in 1709. The reredos by Grinling Gibbons - his bills for £100 exist (Guildhall Library, MS, 3925) - is a splendid composition of double Corinthian columns supporting a broken pediment enriched with limewood carvings. The gilded pelican with nest and offspring are gilded. This small domed building, bombed in 1940, and restored carefully (1948-53), is among the most attractive of Wren's City churches.

144 THE MONUMENT, Detail of base and panel, 1677.
The carved panel by Caius Gabriel Cibber represents 'Charles II succouring the City of London after the Great Fire'. The monument was erected 1671-77 to the designs of Wren and Hooke to commemorate the awesome event. The Monument was engraved by Hulsburgh in 1724.
Lit: *Wren Soc.* **XVIII:** pl. 18.

THE MONUMENT, *see also* pl. 43.

145 COAT-OF-ARMS of Sir Christopher Wren, oil on board, *c* 1675. Loaned to the Royal Hospital, Chelsea.
Although the date of Wren's knighthood is given variously as 1672 or 1674 his right to bear arms is commemorated in this splendid painting. The heraldic descriptions are:
Arms Argent a chevron between three lions' heads erased Azure langued Gules on a chief of the last three cross crosslets Or.
Crest A lion's head as in the arms pierced through the neck from the dexter by a broken spear embrued Proper.
Motto: Numero pondere et mensura. (I reckon by weight and measure.)

146 ST DUNSTAN-IN-THE-EAST. 1670-71, Steeple 1697-99.
The shell of an old church was incorporated in Wren's conception, and he provided a Gothic steeple, which owed its inspiration to the pre-Fire steeple of St Mary-le-Bow. The nave and chancel were rebuilt in the early 1820s. Miraculously the steeple survived the bombing which destroyed the church in 1941.

147 'A PROSPECT OF THE CITY OF LONDON'. early 18th century. *Guildhall Library, London* (Photograph: Library).
St Paul's Cathedral and 50 towers, spires, and other City landmarks are numbered on this large prospect, which is titled in French and Latin. It depicted what was true in post-Fire London, the dominance of St Paul's, the new churches and the active trade on the river.

148 ST MARY-LE-BOW, Study for east elevation, *c* 1671. ASC, Oxford I/72 (Photograph: ASC).
When thinking of individual designs for the rebuilding of the City churches it was inevitable that Wren should use certain features from one in another. The circular lights were used at St Dionis and the triangular pediments of the

windows at St Mary Aldermanbury. While there may still have been some immaturity at this early date none is found in the handling of the adjacent tower and spire (*see* pls. 153-154).

149 ST ANTHOLIN, Watling Street, Study for steeple, *c* 1682. ASC, Oxford II/49 (Photograph: ASC).
Wren first designed a domed turret for St Antholin, which had connections with his lovely design for the tower of St Benet Fink (a church demolished in 1842-44 for the erection of the Royal Exchange). Whether he was persuaded to changes by the Vestry members or of his own accord is not known. However St Antholin was given a more elaborate design. The church was demolished in 1875, a fragment of the spire, renewed in 1825, survives.
Lit: Furst. 1956: 64: Colvin H M. *A Biographical Dictionary of British Architects, 1600-1840*. London, 1978: 928.

150 ST JAMES'S. Westminster, (Piccadilly), Elevation study, *c* 1675. ASC, Oxford II/45 (Photograph: ASC).
While there seems little connection between this design and that for St Antholin (*see* pl. 149), the lantern above the domical capping is identical to that at the base of the St Antholin steeple. The small dome was intended to be covered with metal scales, but the design was not carried out (*see also* pl. 183).

151-152 ST MAGNUS THE MARTYR, Tower and lantern from the north-east, 1671-76, steeple completed 1705; Interior looking east.
The inventiveness of the architect, and the competence of his office were tested in this fine church. Wren turned to the Jesuit church at Antwerp for his model, and a drawing of that survived in the Bute collection of drawings from his office (Sotheby's 23 May 1951, lot 10/32). The form of the tower changes from square to octagon, with the lead cupola and lantern, topped by a spire, or it is as Professor Downes accurately describes: 'the monumental pepperpot of St Magnus'.
    The church is divided into nave and aisles by the tall Ionic columns. The altarpiece is one of the finest in the City, and there are splendid fittings, including the pulpit with tester and a 'sumptuous west gallery'.
Lit: Clarke B F L, *Parish Churches of London*, London, 1966: 30-31.

153-154 ST MARY-LE-BOW, Doorway at base of Tower, 1672, and the engraved source by François Mansart, *c* 1645, engraved by J F Blondel *L'architecture françoise*, 1752-56, (Photograph: Birmingham Reference Library (**154**).)
The lowest storey of the tower of St Mary-le-Bow has a splendid door with Doric columns supporting an entablature, surmounted by two boys. The great niche with channelled voussoirs gives a dominance to the whole. The idea seems to have been taken from François Mansart's door for the Hôtel de Conti in Paris but with altered proportions and the use of Doric columns. Thomas Cartwright and Colin Thompson were paid for 'ye Great Neech' in March 1672. (*see also* pls. 139-140).

155 ST MARY-LE-BOW, Plan of the Church.

156 ST BRIDE, Fleet Street, Plan of the Church.

157 ST BRIDE, Fleet Street, 1671-78, steeple 1701-03.
Wren's first many-storeyed steeple was for the church of St Mary-le-Bow (*see* pl. 139) - the remainder are later in date. The belfry stage of the tower has pilasters flanking the round-headed windows, with engaged columns at the corners. The segmental pediments rise towards the four octagonal storeys, and the upper octagonal pyramid. The centre of the steeple, ingeniously, houses an open stone staircase.

158 ST BRIDE, Fleet Street, Interior looking east, 1671-78, restored 1955-57.
Coupled Doric columns divide the Nave from the aisles. The Nave has a tunnel vault with clerestory windows cut into it. This photograph is prior to the restoration by W Godfrey Allen, 1955-57, following the 1940 bombing. The galleries were not replaced and the seating altered - the box pews shown here are those done by William Cleer and William Gray. The glass in the east window was put in by Basil Champneys (1842-1935).

159 ST MARY ALDERMANBURY. Interior looking east; 1670-76; amended 1864, 1923; bombed 1940, re-erected at Fulton, Missouri, USA, 1964-65.
This pre-war photograph shows the tunnel vault ceiling, plastered by John Grove and the joinery

by William Cleer. The tracery and glass in the east window, together with other amendments were done in 1864. The church was re-erected in America as a memorial to Sir Winston Churchill.

160 ST BENET, Paul's Wharf, 1677-83 (now the Welsh Church).
The variety in tower and spire is continued here by a small lead cupola with a lantern, set above a brick and stone three-stage tower. The masons were Thomas and Edward Strong.

161 ST EDMUND KING AND MARTYR, Lombard Street, 1670-79, spire completed after 1708. ASC, Oxford II/44 (Photograph: ASC).
This drawing is signed in the pediment by Wren with his cypher, and is a useful example of the architect's work before he left most of these matters to his busy drafting office. The design dates from the very early 1670s and the church was intended to fit a long narrow site, so that the tower, steeple and porch became the principal (south) front.
Lit: Furst. 1956: 16.

162-163 ST JAMES GARLICKHYTHE, Garlick Hill, 1676-83, spire 1713-17, repaired 1838. Exterior from the west (**162**); Interior looking east (**163**).
The attractive steeple on this church is in several stages, with projecting Ionic columns at the angles of the lower one. The mason was Edward Strong jnr, and its cost was £1559. 19s 11d. There have been many repairs in the 19th century, but a great deal of good interior woodwork survives. This photograph shows the Victorian glass, which was removed in the repairs of 1954-63 following bomb damage, and that from death-watch beetle.

164 ST MARGARET LOTHBURY, 1686-90, altered 1890-91. Interior looking east.
The splendid screen came from the demolished church of All Hallows', Upper Thames Street, and was the gift of Theodore Jacobsen. It has open twisted balusters. Many other demolished churches were the source of other fittings; the tester of the pulpit again from All Hallows', and the communion table and altarpiece from St Olave's, Old Jewry. James Elmes in his *Life* of Wren (1823), said that the church 'faces Mr Soane's new front of the Bank of England, and is not disgraced by its modern neighbour'.

165-167 ALL HALLOWS, Lombard Street, 1686-94, demolished 1939. Interior looking east (**165**); Altarpiece (**166**); Pulpit (**167**).
With a carpenter, four joiners, and two carvers at work under Wren it was inevitable that the woodwork of this church was exceptionally fine. Although the City Corporation and a number of learned societies opposed the proposal to demolish put to the Privy Council by the Ecclesiastical Commission it was approved. The tower and fittings were re-erected as part of All Hallows, Twickenham.
Lit: Colvin H M. *A Biographical Dictionary of British Architects, 1600-1840.* London 1978: 928.

168 ST MARY ALDERMARY, South aisle vault, 1682, (Photograph: National Monuments Record).
The plasterwork, by Henry Doogood in the Gothic style copies early 17th century work formerly in the Church. Recent research has established that Henry Rogers, a wealthy Somerset squire, left money at his death in 1672 to be used under his niece Anne's supervision in 'the building of a church in London where was most need'. After winning a lawsuit against her fellow executors Anne Rogers applied the money to restore St Mary Aldermary. Wren's connection with the church is tenuous. His deputy at St Paul's, John Oliver, was in charge of work. He may have executed Wren's design, or provided one himself. There is no doubt, however, of Wren's involvement on the repair of the tower, 1701-03 (*see also* pl. 182). His assistant, William Dickinson, who interested himself in Gothic, designed the upper stages under the Surveyor-General's direction.
Lit: Colvin H M. The Church of St Mary Aldermary and its rebuilding after the Great Fire of London. *Architectural History.* 1981; 24: 24-31.

169-170 ST ANDREW, Holborn 1684-90, tower completed 1703. Exterior, looking west (**169**); Pulpit (**170**); (Photograph: National Monuments Record (**170**).
This church had escaped the Great Fire and was rebuilt by Wren. The 15th century tower was faced and heightened. The church was gutted by bombing, but the tower and walls survived. The contents were all destroyed. Fortunately the fine pulpit (**170**) by Edward Pierce had been photographed prior to that time.

171-172 ST MARTIN, Ludgate, Elevation study, ASC, Oxford II/50, and Exterior, south elevation, 1677-84, (Photograph: ASC (**171**).

The church has followed the drawing, a situation not always practised or apparent. Christopher Kempster the mason built the church to Wren's design. The front is to the south, with the tower projecting slightly, and ogee scrolls connecting it with other bays. The ogee dome, balcony, lantern and spire are covered with lead.

173 ST STEPHEN, Walbrook, Engraving by John Bowles of interior, *c* 1755. *Guildhall Library, London* (Photograph: Library).

The disposition of columns and the control of the domed interior space have been referred to previously (*see* pl. 142). It is rendered most effectively in this axial view.

174 ST MICHAEL, PATERNOSTER ROYAL 1686-94, steeple completed 1713.

The steeple is similar to that of St James, Garlickhythe (*see* pl. 162), but the stages are octagonal rather than square. The projecting columns at the angles are set singly at the angles. Edward Strong jnr, was the mason. His father had worked on Wren's rebuilding of the church in the 1680s. Some of the interior fittings of the church were brought from All Hallows', Thames Street (*see also* pl.175).

175 ALL HALLOWS THE GREAT, Upper Thames Street, 1677-83, demolished 1893-94. Pulpit *c* 1685 (Photograph: National Monuments Record).

The distribution of the fine fittings at the church's demolition enriched the churches of St Margaret, Lothbury (*see* pl. 164), St Michael, Paternoster Royal, and All Hallows, Gospel Oak. St Paul's, Hammersmith now houses the pulpit, which was carved by Thomas Powell and William Cleer.

176 CHRIST CHURCH, Newgate Street (right). Engraving of Christ's Hospital (1692-), and the church (1677-87), *Guildhall Library, London* (Photograph: Library).

Wren had some connection with the design for the Writing School of Christ's Hospital, of which he was a governor, but Hawksmoor was much more involved. However this engraving is illustrated to indicate the contemporary position of his church (*see* pl. 178).

Lit: Pearce E H *Annals of Christ's Hospital* London, 1908: 2nd edn.

177 ST ANDREW-BY-THE-WARDROBE, Queen Victoria Street, 1685-93. Exterior, south elevation (pre-1939).

This church, which gained a dominant position when Queen Victoria Street was made, was a tribute to Wren's bricklayer, Thomas Horn. The south front and tower, although amended in 1875, are well proportioned and 'convenient'. This illustration dates from prior to its bombing in 1940, and its restoration (1959-61) by Marshall Sisson.

178 CHRIST CHURCH, Newgate Street, 1677-87, steeple completed 1701-04.

This impressive tower with its segmental pediments, and the diminishing stages of the steeple, with the other walls, survived bombing in the Second World War. The church has however remained unrestored. The steeple was completed by Edward Strong jnr.

179-180 ST SWITHIN, Cannon Street, 1677-85, demolished after bombing, 1941.

Joshua Marshall and Samuel Fulkes, experienced masons at St Paul's built this interesting little church with its eight-sided dome. The font cover (**180**), seemingly by the carver Richard Cleere, is now at St Ethelburga's, Bishopsgate, but this pre-war photograph was taken in St Swithin's itself.

181 ST PETER UPON CORNHILL, East elevation, 1675-81.

This grand east front, by the masons Joshua Marshall and Abraham Story, shows how Wren could present the best elevation to the street, with a 'homely exterior' elsewhere. Story had visited Holland in 1674 and told Robert Hooke about churches in Amsterdam, which were influential on the design of some London churches by Wren; St Anne and St Agnes, St Mary at Hill, and St Martin, Ludgate. It is presumed Hooke drew attention to them, and Story also worked under Hooke at the Royal College of Physicians, and, in addition to St Peter upon Cornhill, at St Edmund, King and Martyr (*see* pl. 161).

182 ST MARY ALDERMARY, Gothic Tower, completed 1701-02.

We have illustrated the Gothic interior of this church (see pl. 168) created 20 years before the tower was complete. The mason was John Clarke, and the design was provided by Wren's clerk, William Dickinson under the Surveyor-General's supervision. The pinnacles were damaged in 1703, and evidences of the various earlier stages of the tower - it was started in 1510, completed in 1629 and burned in the Great Fire - were lost by refacing in Portland stone early in the present century.

183 ST JAMES'S CHURCH, Westminster (Piccadilly) 1676-84, restored 1947-54. Interior looking west.

This church, beyond the City, and undamaged by the Great Fire, suffered grievously in the Second World War. The church was built by Wren at the expense of Henry Jermyn, Earl of St Albans, and was consecrated on 13 July 1684. The galleries rest on square piers, with Corinthian columns above. The original plasterwork was probably by Henry Doogood. The organ by Renatus Harris, was that made for the Roman Catholic Chapel of Whitehall Palace. It was given to the church in 1691 by Queen Mary II. The church was badly damaged by bombing in 1940, but was restored, faithfully, by Sir Albert Richardson.

184-185 ST CLEMENT DANES, Strand, Westminster, 1680-82, upper stage of Tower, 1719-20. Elevation study, ASC, Oxford II/55; the church from the west (Photograph: ASC (**184**).

St Clement's was not touched by the Great Fire, but as it was in bad condition it was taken down, except for the tower. Then Wren rebuilt it entirely. He designed an aisled basilican church to fit a difficult site. Wren gave his design free, but ample funds existed to build the church in Portland stone.

The Vestry came to an agreement in 1719 that the tower should be raised 7½ metres (25ft), with an ornamental steeple of not less than 15 metres (50ft). James Gibbs designed this and William Townesend built the three stages in the Ionic, Corinthian and Composite orders.

186 WESTMINSTER ABBEY, Drawing, elevation of North Transept, drawn 1719, and approved by Wren, 20 May 1719. *Westminster Abbey Library* (Photograph: Library).

This restoration project occupied Wren in his late years. His knowledge of Gothic forms was not often put to use. He had had sympathy however with the style from his early dealings with Old St Paul's. He submitted, (but at the advanced age of 87 did not presumably execute), a design 'of a Style with the Rest of the Structure'. It had attached flaps which when raised showed the intended alterations. His approbation of it, with a somewhat trembling hand, is shown by his signature in the top left corner, under the words 'I doe Approve of this Design'.

187-189 INGESTRE CHURCH, Staffordshire, 1673-76. Exterior from the south-west (**187**); Interior looking east (**188**); the Pulpit (**189**), (Photographs: National Monuments Record).

Wren may have designed this attractive Caroline church for his fellow-member of the Royal Society, Walter Chetwynd. An elevation for a lantern on a tower, inscribed 'Mr Chetwin's Tower' (which was not executed) was sold in the Bute collection (Sotheby's, 23 May 1951, lot no. 17/8). The church may however have been designed by someone associated with Wren's office.

Domestic Architecture

190 WINSLOW HALL, Buckinghamshire, 1699-1702.

William Lowndes, Secretary of the Treasury to William III may have asked Wren to design his house, Winslow Hall. The architect examined the workmen's bills, but as Dr H M Colvin notes 'the fact that he performed this service does not prove that he was the architect'.

191 TRING MANOR HOUSE, Hertfordshire, *c* 1670, demolished 19th century. (Photograph: Birmingham Reference Library).

This engraving, taken from Chauncy's *Historical Antiquities of Hertfordshire,* (1700) is dedicated to its owner Henry Guy by John Oliver, Assistant Surveyor at St Paul's Cathedral. Roger North stated that it had been 'built by Sr Chr Wren'. Lit: Colvin H M. *A Biographical Dictionary of British Architects, 1600-1840.* London. 1978: 925.

192 MARLBOROUGH HOUSE, St James's, London, 1709-11. Engraving of the 'South-

West Prospect' by James Lightbody, *c* 1711. *Guildhall Library, London* (Photograph: Library). The first Duke of Marlborough asked Wren (assisted by his son) to design this London house. There have been many additions to it in the 18th and 19th centuries. A letter in the British Library (BL MS 9123, f. 212), indicates that the Duke laid stress 'upon the Employing Sr Chr Wren to build the house'. Colen Campbell's *Vitruvius Britannicus* (**I**, 1715) also stated that 'The design was given by Mr Wren' and (p. 40) 'Invented by Christopher Wren Esq.'. The foundation stones of Marlborough House were laid by the Duchess of Marlborough, on 24 May and 4 June 1709. Lit: Green D. *Blenheim Palace,* London, 1951: 248-249.

Memorabilia

193 LETTER from Wren to his father, January 1641. In the heirloom copy of *Parentalia* (hereafter BL *Parentalia*). British Architectural Library, London (Photograph: Library).
Before leaving home for Westminster School the young nine-year-old Christopher Wren wrote a letter to his father in Latin. It expressed his gratitude 'for things in general'.

194 DESIGN FOR A WEATHER-CLOCK, by Christopher Wren. In BL *Parentalia, c* 1647 (Photograph: as for pl. 193).
This is another example of Wren's youthful precocity and an indication of his obsession with scientific problems. *Parentalia* also contains drawings showing the anatomy of the river eel, and the working of the deaf-and-dumb language.

195 WREN'S INAUGURAL ORATION, at Gresham College, 1657. In BL *Parentalia* (Photograph: as for pl. 193).
Wren was 25 years old when he gave the inaugural oration on his appointment as Professor of Astronomy at Gresham College. This is the opening page in Latin.

196 SIR CHRISTOPHER WREN, 1632-1723. Marble bust by Edward Pierce, *c* 1673. *Ashmolean Museum, Oxford* (Photograph: Museum).
This spirited Baroque bust, a detail of which is shown elsewhere (*see* Frontispiece) was by Edward Pierce (*c*1635-95), one of Wren's most

talented carvers in wood and stone. He worked at several of the City Churches, and was the son of a decorative painter. The bust may have been a present on Wren's knighthood, and probably owes something to Wren's own suggestions. He had, after all, seen Bernini's bust of Louis XIV at an early stage when he was in Paris in 1665. A plaster copy is at All Souls College, Oxford.

197 LETTER, from Sir Christopher Wren to his future wife, Faith Coghill, *c* 1668. In BL, *Parentalia* (Photograph: as for pl. 193).
Wren's letter is a reply to Faith's request that he arrange the repair of a watch she had dropped into the sea. It starts: 'Madam - The artificer having never before mett with a drowned Watch; like an ignorant physician has been soe long about the cure that he hath made me very unquiet that your comands should be soe long deferred: however I have sent the Watch at last, and envie the felicity of it, that it should be soe near your side ...'.

198 DRAWING OF A HAND, by Christopher Wren inscribed 'An arte to make The Dumb to speake. The Deafe to heare. To speake amongst others unheard or understande. Learnd in an hour'. In BL *Parentalia* (Photograph: Library).

199 SIR CHRISTOPHER WREN, 1632-1723. Painting, oil on canvas, 184 × 175 cm, *c* 1706-24. *The Sheldonian Theatre, Oxford* (Photograph: Thomas Photos, Oxford).
This fine canvas was begun by Antonio Verrio, and at his death in 1707 finished by Sir Godfrey Kneller and Sir James Thornhill. It is so inscribed at the foot in Latin. Wren is shown holding a plan of St Paul's, a drawing of the Sheldonian Theatre at his feet, and St Paul's and the City painted in the left distance. The painting is a fascinating 'iconographical document'. There is a copy by Joseph Smith (1828) at Wadham College, Oxford.

200 SIR CHRISTOPHER WREN, 1632-1723, Painting, by Sir Godfrey Kneller, oil on canvas, 122 × 97 cm, s & d, 1711. *National Portrait Gallery, London,* No. 113 (Photograph: Gallery).
This well-known portrait, of which copies exist at St Paul's Deanery and All Souls College, Oxford, shows the Surveyor-General with a pair of dividers in his right hand above a plan of St Paul's Cathedral (*see also* pl. 202).

201 SIR CHRISTOPHER WREN, 1632-1723, Drawing, by Henry Cooke, pen and brush and blue ink, heightened in white, 41 × 29 cm, *c* 1683 *Museum Boymans - van Beuningen, Rotterdam* (Photograph: Museum).
This drawing was engraved in reverse between 1723 and 1742 by E Kirkhall after Closterman's portrait of Wren at The Royal Society (*see* pl. 136).
Lit: Royal Academy catalogue, *The Age of Charles II*, London, 1960-61; 215.

202 SIR CHRISTOPHER WREN, 1632-1723, Detail of portrait by Sir Godfrey Kneller, 1711, *National Portrait Gallery, London* (Photograph: Gallery).
Detail of portrait reproduced as pl. 200.

203 SIR CHRISTOPHER WREN, 1632-1723, Portrait relief, by David Le Marchand, ivory, bust profile to right, 12 × 8.5 cm, *c* 1723 *National Portrait Gallery, London.* No. 4500 (Photograph: Gallery).
This profile was sold at Sotheby's 4 July 1966, (lot 54) as 'unknown man'. It was purchased by the National Portrait Gallery on identification as Sir Christopher Wren. The profile was copied by the Wedgwood factory in the 18th and 19th centuries.

204 JANE WREN, 1678-1704, Marble relief, St Paul's Cathedral, Crypt.
In February 1677 Wren married for the second time. His bride was Jane the daughter of Lord Fitzwilliam of Lifford. They had two children, Jane and William. Jane, Wren's favourite, died at the age of twenty-six. The marble relief shows her seated at an organ, for she was dedicated to music.

205 CHRISTOPHER WREN, Jnr, 1675-1747, Engraving by Isaac Faber, 1750. *National Portrait Gallery, London* (Photograph: Gallery).
Christopher Wren jnr, Wren's eldest son was born to the architect's first wife, Faith Coghill. He was also an architect, holding the post of Chief Clerk to the King's Works from 1702 until 1716. He was dismissed due to the reforms of the Earl of Halifax. He made the collection of family documents which was published by his son Stephen in 1750 as *Parentalia: Memoirs of the Family of the Wrens.* The heirloom copy of this is at the British Architectural Library, London.
Lit: Weaver L. 'The Interleaved Copy of Wren's *Parentalia,* with manuscript insertions, *Royal Institute of British Architects Journal, 1911;* **XVIII:** 16; 3rd ser.

206 DEATH MASK OF SIR CHRISTOPHER WREN, Plaster, 1723. *All Souls College, Oxford* (Photograph: ASC).
This death mask was bequeathed to the College by Miss Wren of Bromley, the great granddaughter of the architect, at her death in 1851.
Lit: Poole R L, *Catalogue of Portraits in ... Oxford.* Oxford (1912-25): Vols 1-3; **II:** 27.

207 TOMB OF SIR CHRISTOPHER WREN, 1723. St Paul's Cathedral, Crypt.
Wren's grave is marked by a simple black slab with a simple inscription: 'Here Lieth Sr Christopher Wren The Builder of this Cathedral Church of St Paul & who Dyed in the year of our LORD, MDCCXXIII And of his Age XCI'. Later his son set up a further Latin inscription to be set up above his grave. It ends: *Lector si monumentum requiris circumspice,* (Reader, if you seek a monument, look around you).

The Plates

▷ 1 Pembroke College, Cambridge, The Chapel, 1663-65

△ **4** The Sheldonian Theatre, Oxford,
1664-69. Engraving by David Loggan, 1675

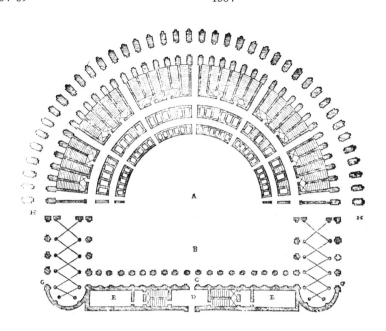

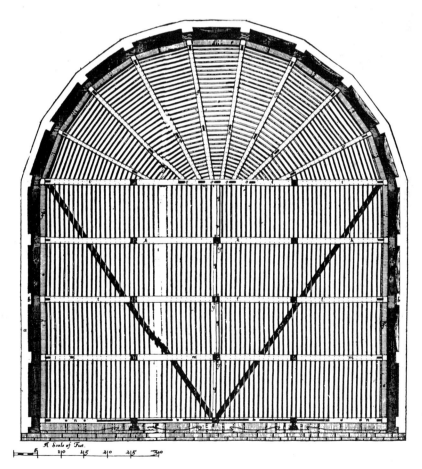

△ 7 The Sheldonian Theatre, Oxford. Plan. Engraving, 1677.

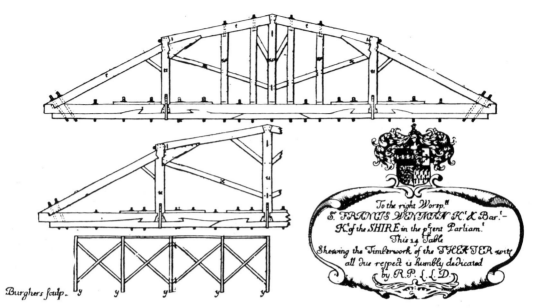

Burghers sculp.

To the right Worsp.ll
S. FRANCIS WENMAN K.t & Bar.t
K.t of the SHIRE in the p.sent Parliam.t
This 14 Table
Shewing the Timberwork of the THEATER with
all due respect is humbly dedicated
by R.P. L.L.D

△ **8** The Sheldonian Theatre, Oxford.
Timber trusses. Engraving, 1677

▽ **9** The Sheldonian Theatre, Oxford.
Engraving of interior by John Buckler, 1815

∇ **10** Emmanuel College, Cambridge, The
Chapel range, 1668-73

△ **11** Interior looking east, *c* 1673

△ **12** Senate House, Cambridge. Elevation
drawing, 1674

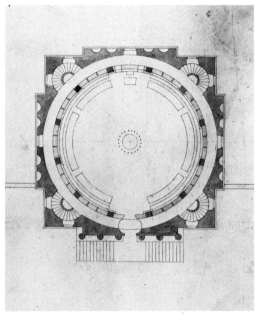

△ **13-14** Trinity College Library, Cambridge. First scheme, elevation and plan, *c* 1674

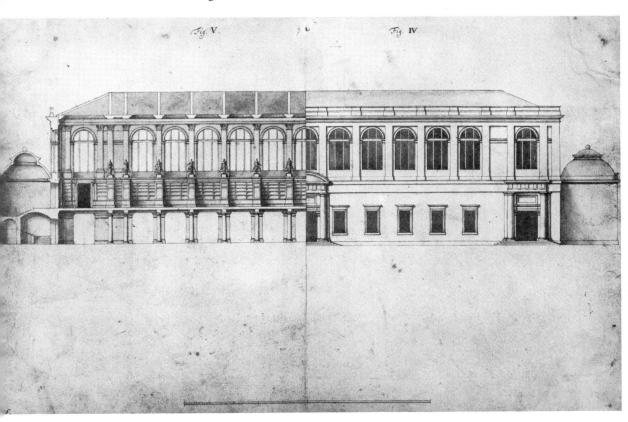

▽ **16** River front, 1676-84

△ **18** Trinity College Library, Cambridge.
Interior, 1676-92

▽ **19** Winchester Palace, Hampshire. Elevation, east court - front, 1682-83

△ **20** Elevation across court front, *c* 1686

▽   **21** Winchester Palace, Hampshire, Drawing 'as Intended to have been finished by Sir Christopher Wren', *c* 1780

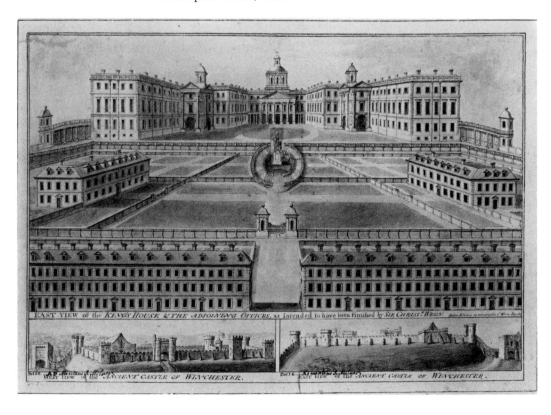

EAST VIEW of the *KING'S HOUSE & THE ADJOINING OFFICES*, as Intended to have been finished by *SIR CHRIST. WREN*.

WEST VIEW of the *ANCIENT CASTLE OF WINCHESTER*.   EAST VIEW of the *ANCIENT CASTLE OF WINCHESTER*.

∇   **22** Whitehall Palace. Part-elevation towards River Thames, 1698

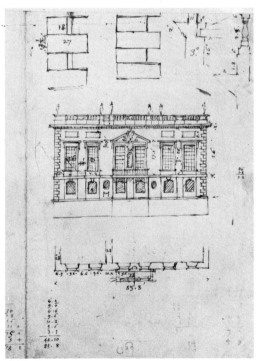

△   **23** Drawing of the Queen's New Apartments, *c* 1688

△   **24** Detail of Queen's New Apartment.
Engraved by Leonard Knyff, *c* 1695-97

∇   **25a** and **b** Whitehall Palace. Second design,
Westminster elevation, 1698

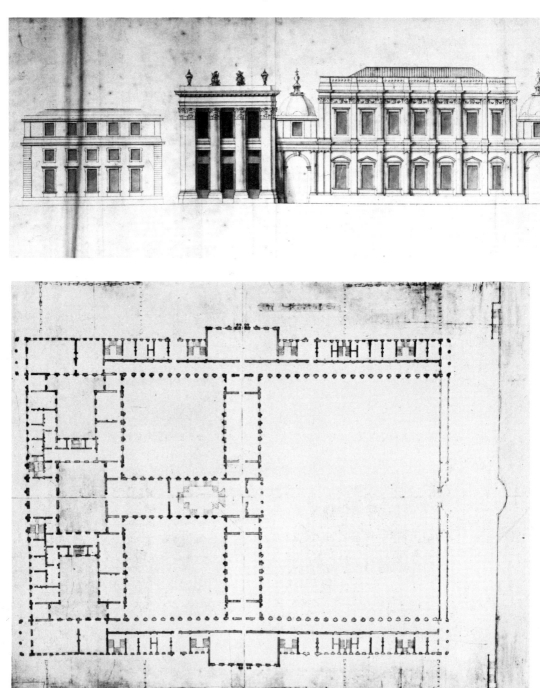

△   **26** Whitehall Palace. Draft plan of the
second design, 1698

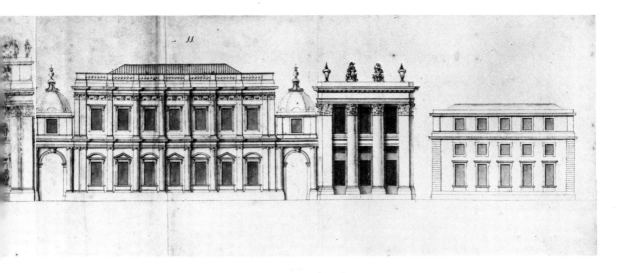

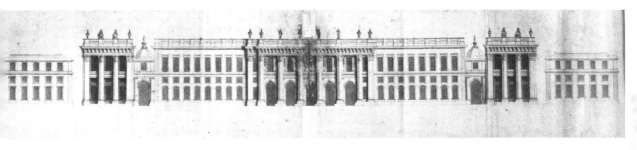

△ **27** Second design, river front, 1698   ▽ **28** Two carved angels formerly in Palace, 1686

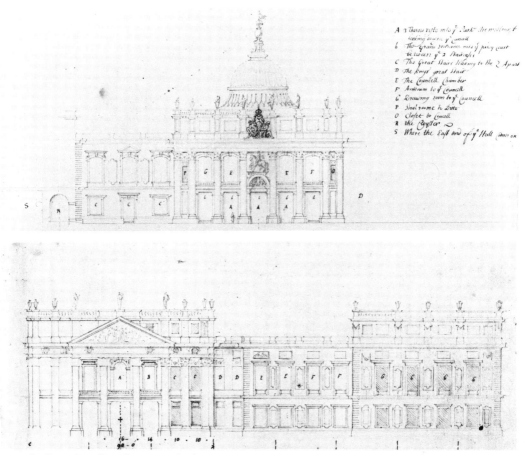

A ꝝ Thorow vista into y⁰ Park the middone ʒ looking towards y⁰ canall
b The Grain entrance into y⁰ privy court between y⁰ 2 staircases
C The Great Stairs leading to the 2 Apart
D The Kings great stair
E The Councell Chamber
F Anteroom to y⁰ Councell
G Drawing room to y⁰ councell
P Dressroome to ditto
O Closet to councell
R the Register
S Where the East end of y⁰ Hall comes on

△ **31** Drawing, first design, park elevation, 1689

∇ **32** Central part of the east front, 1689-1702

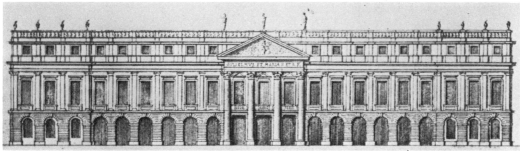

△ **33** Final design for the east front, 1689

△   **35** Hampton Court Palace. Detail of a
panel in the Fountain Screen by Jean Tijou,
c 1693

▷   **36** Hampton Court Palace. The King's
Staircase, 1701-02

△ **37** Hampton Court Palace, The King's Staircase, 1702-02

▽ **38** Hampton Court Palace. The King's Bedroom, ceiling, 1701

△ **39** The King's Bedroom, *c* 1700

The Royal Palace of Kensington   Le Palais Royal de Kensington

△   40 Kensington Palace, London. Engraving by Henry Overton, *c* 1720

▽   41 The south front, 1695-96

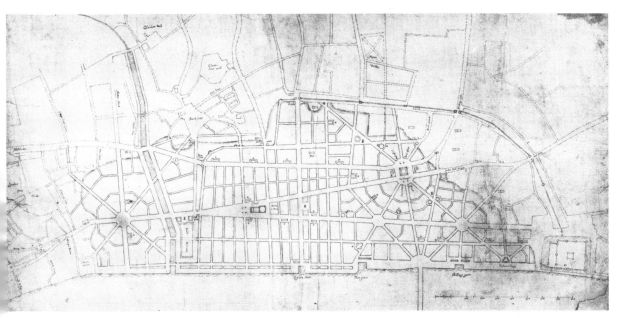

△ **42** Plan for the City of London, 1666

◁ **43** The Monument, London, 1671-77

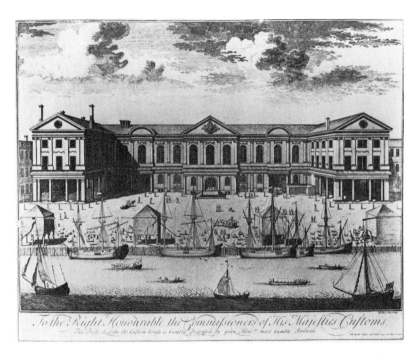

To the Right Honourable the Commissioners of His Majesty's Customs.
This Prospect of the the Custom house is humbly Presented by your Honours most humble Servants

△　**44**　The London Custom House, 1669-71.
Engraved by John Harris, 1714

△　**45**　Greenwich, Kent, The Royal Hospital
for Seamen. First scheme, perspective, 1694

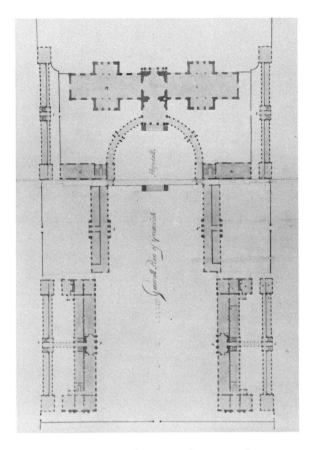

△ **46** Greenwich Hospital. First scheme, plan, 1694

▽ **47** Model, 1699

∇ **48** Greenwich Hospital. Drawing, river
elevation and Great Hall, 1696

∇ **49** Greenwich Hospital. Engraving, *c* 1700

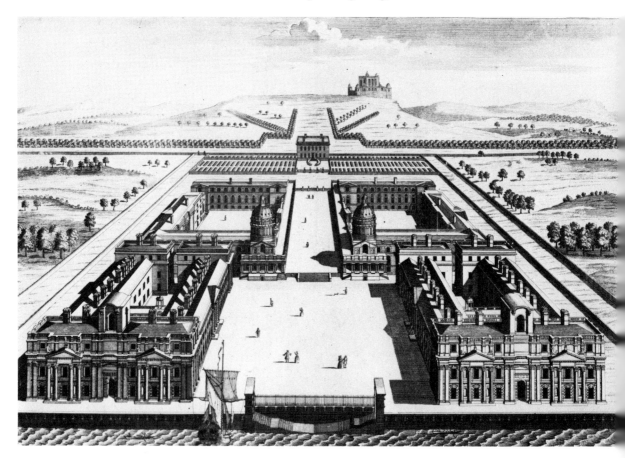

▽ **50** Greenwich Hospital. The King William Block, west elevation, 1696-1707

▽ **51** The King William Block, from river terrace, 1698-1704

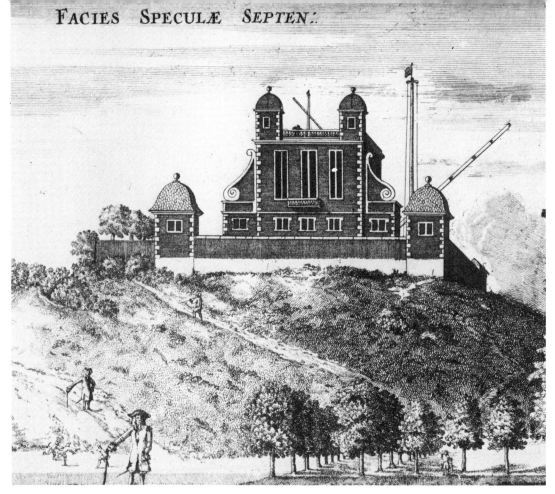

△ **52** The Royal Observatory, Greenwich.
Engraved by Francis Place, *c* 1676

△ **53** The Royal Observatory, Greenwich,
1675

△▽ **54-55** Lincoln Cathedral Library. Interior, and detail of its doorway, 1674-75

∇   56 Chelsea, The Royal Hospital. Detail
of layout. Engraved by Johannes Kip, 1694

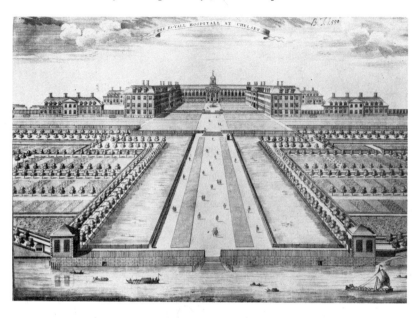

△   57 Chelsea Hospital. Figure Court,
North Portico, 1682-89

▷   58 Chelsea Hospital. The east wing,
1689-92

△ **59** Windsor, Berkshire. The Court House, 1698

▽ **60** Queen Mary II. Design by Grinling Gibbons for her monument, 1695

▷ **61** The Sheldonian Theatre, Oxford, 1664-69

△ **62** The Sheldonian Theatre, Oxford. Interior, 1664-69

▷ **63** Tom Tower, Christ Church, Oxford, upper part by Wren, begun 1681

△　64 Hampton Court Palace. The east　▽　65 The South front, 1689-1702
front, 1689-1702

▷　66 Hampton Court Palace. The Fountain
Court, 1689-1702

△　67 Greenwich Hospital. From the River
Thames, 1698-1707

▷　68 Greenwich Hospital. The Painted
Hall, 1702-17

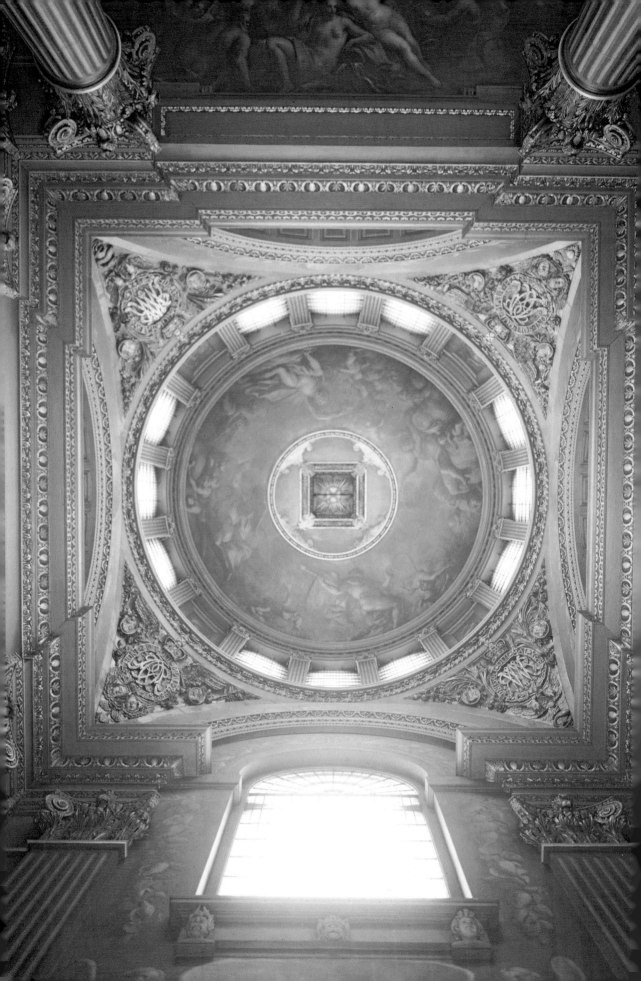

◁ **69** Greenwich Hospital, The Painted Hall, looking towards the ceiling

△ **70** The Painted Hall. Detail of the ceiling

◁ **71** Chelsea Hospital, London. Central part of the north front, 1682-89

△ **72** St Paul's Cathedral, London. From the south-east, 1675-1710

◁ **73** St Paul's Cathedral. The west front,
1690-1708

△ **74** The North West Tower from the
roof, 1705

△ **75** St Paul's Cathedral. South Transept front, 1698-1700

▷ **76** The Dome, seen from the roof of the Nave, 1704-08

△   **77** St Paul's Cathedral. Painting of north
and west elevations by Canaletto, *c* 1754

△ **78** Old St Paul's Church, London. Etching by Wenceslaus Hollar, 1656

▽ **79** Ruins, drawn by Thomas Wyck, *c*1672

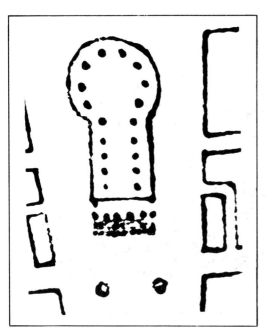

80 St Paul's Cathedral, London. Detail from the City of London Plan, 1666

81 Detail from the City of London Plan, 1666

82 Pre-Fire Design, 1666

△ **83** St Paul's Cathedral. First Model, 1670   ▽ **84** 'Greek Cross Design', elevation, 1673

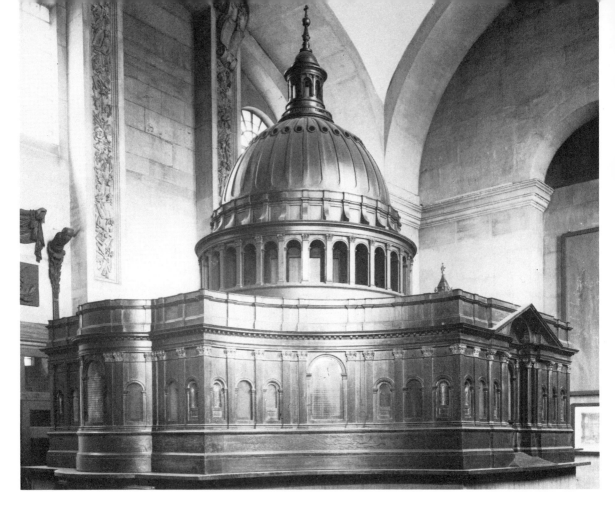

△ 85 St Paul's Cathedral. The 'Great Model' from the north-west, 1673-74

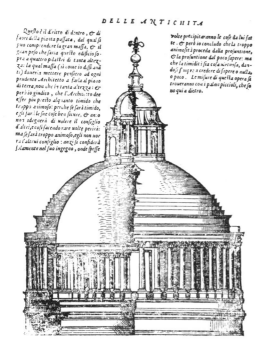

△ 86 St Peter's Basilica, Rome. Design for the Dome by Donato Bramante. Engraved by Serlio, 1584

△ 87 Design for the Dome by Michelangelo Engraved by Du Perac, 1568-69

△ **88** St Paul's Cathedral, London. The 'Great Model', interior, 1673-74

▽ **89** The 'Great Model' Design, 1673. Engraved by Henry Hulsburgh, *c* 1713

⊲ **90** St Paul's Cathedral. The 'Warrant Design' west elevation, 1675

▽ **91** The 'Warrant Design', south elevation, 1675

△ **92** The 'Warrant Design', section, 1675

△ **93** St Paul's Cathedral. Study of west
elevation, 1702

△   **94** St Paul's Cathedral. Detail of west
elevation, engraved by Simon Gribelin, 1702

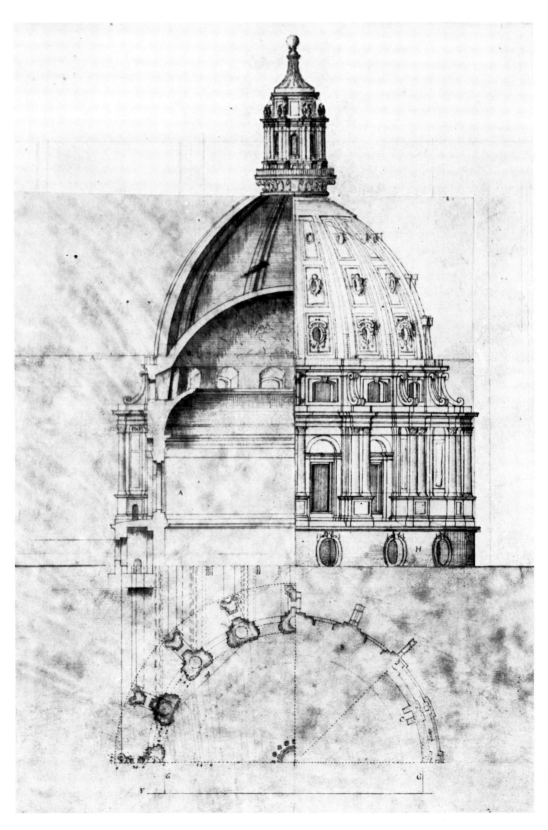

◁　　**95** Mausoleum for King Charles I. Drawing of elevation, 1678

△　　**96** St Paul's Cathedral. Drawing, Dome
Study, *c* 1697

◁ △ **97-98** St Paul's Cathedral. Working drawing for the peristyle of the Dome, *c* 1703, and **98**, as executed, 1703-04

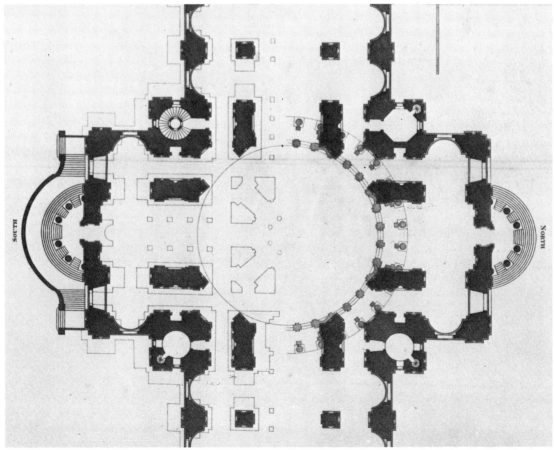

△ **99-100** St Paul's Cathedral. Plan of pavement design, *c* 1703, and same area on ground
plan, *c* 1750

△ **101** St Paul's Cathedral. Back of Screen wall showing the buttresses above the aisle roof

▽ **102** West towers, half elevation and section, *c* 1702

▷ **103** St Paul's Cathedral. West front, Engraved by Henry Hulsburgh, 1713

Western Prospect of St PAULS CHURCH with the Queens Statue

...d on the Thanksgiving Day for ÿ Generall PEACE in ÿ Year 1713.   Printed & Sold by Ph...
St Dunstans Church in Fl...

△▽ **104-105** St Paul's Cathedral. South and west elevations

▷ **106** St Paul's Cathedral. North-east elevation

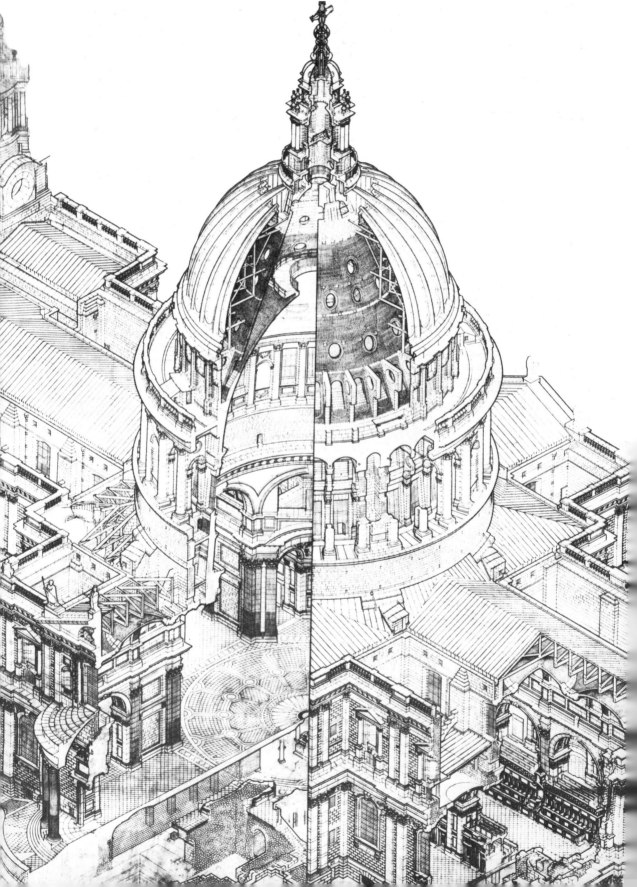

107 St Paul's Cathedral. Isometric section of the Dome. Detail of a drawing by R B Brook-Greaves and W Godfrey Allen

△▽ **108-109** St Paul's Cathedral. The South West Tower from the Golden Gallery, and **109.** Detail of the North West Tower

△ **110** St Paul's Cathedral. Interior of the
choir. Engraved by Robert Trevitt, 1706

▽ **111** Interior looking to the Choir. Engraved *c* 1720

▷ **112** St Paul's Cathedral. Section. Engraved
by Samuel Wale and John Gwynn, 1755

△ ▽ **113-114** St Paul's Cathedral, looking into
the inner painted Dome. Painted by Sir James
Thornhill, 1714-17

△ ▷ **115-116** St Paul's Cathedral. Inner dome. Two engravings of the painted decoration, *c* 1720

▽ ▽ **117-118** St Paul's Cathedral, The inner Dome, construction

◁   **119** St Paul's Cathedral. Circular staircase, South West Tower, completed 1705

△   **120** St Paul's Cathedral. Wrought-iron
gates on south side of Choir, by Jean Tijou,
1698

△   **121** St Paul's Cathedral. Wood screen at rear of Choir Stalls, south Choir aisle, 1698

▽   **122** St Paul's Cathedral. The Choir Stalls, north side, 1696-97

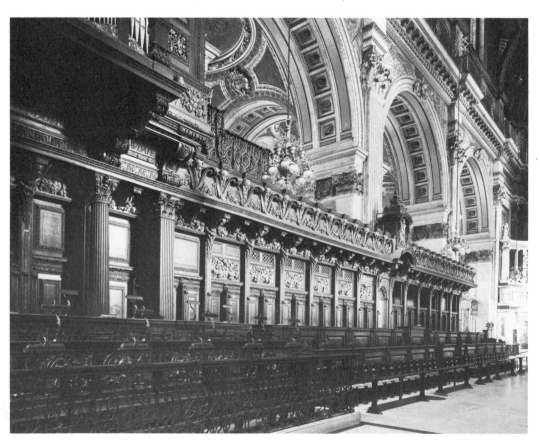

△ ▽ **123-124** St Paul's Cathedral, The Choir
Stalls, north side, 1696-97

The Infide of the Choir of y̆ Cathedral Church of St Paul's LONDON | Chori Ecclefiæ Cathedralis Divi Pauli afpectus Interior.

London Printed for Robt Sayer, Map & Printseller near Serjeants Inn Fleet Street

△   **125** St Paul's Cathedral. Interior of the choir. Engraved by Bernard Lens and Johannes Kip, *c* 1720

△　126 St Paul's Cathedral. The Library Gallery

◁ **127** St Paul's Cathedral. A detail of plasterwork on the Library pilasters

△ **128** St Paul's Cathedral. The Nave, looking east

▷ **129** The North Transept

△ **130** St Paul's Cathedral. The Choir and
High Altar, from the Crossing

▷ **131** The Crossing and the Choir

bishop throne

◁ **132** St Paul's Cathedral. The Choir, looking east

△ **133** The Choir stalls, north side, 1696-97

◁ △ **134-135** St Paul's Cathedral. The
Library, and a detail **135** of one of the carved
wood brackets by Jonathan Maine

CHRISTOPHER WREN KC
DENT OF THE ROYAL
SOCIETY

◁ **136** Sir Christopher Wren, Portrait, *c* 1683 by Johann Baptist Closterman

△ **137** St Vedast, Foster Lane, 1670-73. Tower completed 1709-12

▷ **138** London, The Thames from the terrace of Somerset House, St Paul's Cathedral in the distance. Painting by Canaletto, *c* 1750-51. (Reproduced by gracious permission of Her Majesty The Queen.) (See overleaf.)

◁ △ **139-140** St Mary-le-Bow, Cheapside, from the south-west, 1670-73. Steeple completed 1680

△   **141** St Lawrence, Jewry, from the east,
1671-77

▷   **142** St Stephen, Walbrook, 1672-79. Interior reconstructed 1951-54

△ **143** St Mary Abchurch, 1681-86. Interior reconstructed 1948-53

▷ **144** The Monument, London. Detail of base and panel, 1677

△ **145** Coat-of-Arms of Sir Christopher Wren

▷ **146** St Dunstan-in-the-East, 1670-71. Steeple, 1697-99

A PROSPECT of the CITY of LONDON.

△ **147** 'A Prospect of the City of London'.
Early 18th-century engraving

▽ **148** St Mary-le-Bow. Drawing; study for
east elevation, *c* 1671

◁　**149** St Antholin, Watling Street. Drawing; study for Steeple, *c* 1682

▽　**150** St James's, Westminster (Piccadilly). Drawing; study for elevation, *c* 1675

△ ▷ **151-152** St Magnus The Martyr. Tower
and Lantern from the north-east, 1671-76.
Steeple, completed 1705, and **152** interior looking east

◁ ▽ **153-154** St Mary-le-Bow. Doorway at base of Tower, 1672, and the engraved source by François Mansart for the Hôtel de Conti, Paris

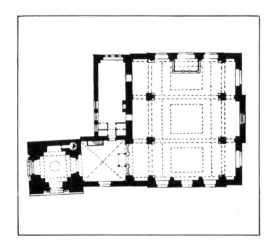

▽ **155** St Mary-le-Bow. Plan of the Church

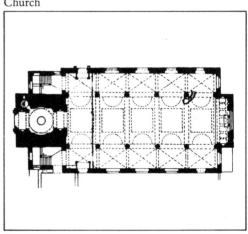

▽ **156** St Bride, Fleet Street. Plan of the Church

▷ **157** St Bride, Fleet Street, 1671-78. Steeple 1701-03

◁ **158** St Bride, Fleet Street. Interior, looking east, 1671-78. Reconstructed 1955-57

△ **159** St Mary Aldermanbury. Interior
looking east, 1670-76. Shown prior to
re-erection in America, 1964-65

◁ **160** St Benet's, Paul's Wharf (now the Welsh Church), 1677-83

△ **161** St Edmund, King and Martyr, Lombard Street, 1670-79. Spire completed after 1708

▷ ▽ **162-163** St James Garlickhythe, Garlick
Hill, 1676-83, spire 1713-17. Exterior, from the
west and **163** interior looking east

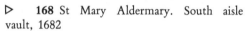

△ ▽ **165-167** All Hallows', Lombard Street, 1686-94. Demolished 1939. Interior, altarpiece and pulpit

▷ **168** St Mary Aldermary. South aisle vault, 1682

◁ ▽ **169-170** St Andrew, Holborn, 1684-90.
Tower completed 1703. Exterior looking west,
and **170** pulpit

◁ △ **171-172** St Martin, Ludgate. Drawing; study for elevation, and **172** exterior, south elevation, 1677-84

△ **173** St Stephen, Walbrook. Engraving of Interior by John Bowles, c 1755

▽ **174** St Michael, Paternoster Royal, 1686-94, Steeple completed 1713

▽ **175** All Hallows the Great, Upper Thames Street, 1677-83. Demolished 1893-94. The Pulpit, *c* 1685

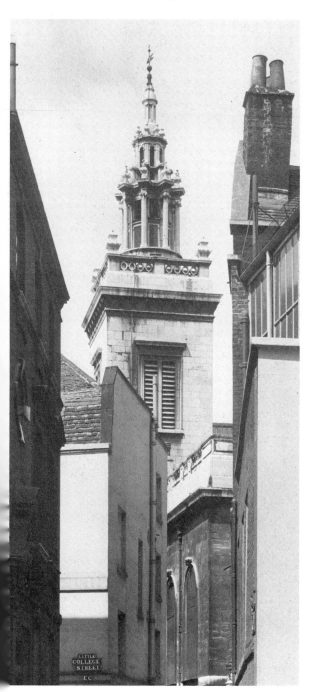

△ **176** Christ Church, Newgate Street, 1677-87, shown in engraving of Christ's Hospital

▽ **177** St Andrew-by-the-Wardrobe, Queen Victoria Street, 1685-93. Exterior, south elevation

∇   **178** Christ Church, Newgate Street,
1677-87. Steeple completed 1701-04

◁ **179** St Swithin, Cannon Street, 1677-85, demolished after bombing, 1941. Exterior

▽ **180** St Swithin, Cannon Street, 1677-85. Font

△ **181** St Peter upon Cornhill. East elevation, 1675-81

▷ **182** St Mary Aldermary. Gothic Tower, completed 1701-02

◁ **183** St James's Church, Westminster (Piccadilly) 1676-84. Reconstructed 1947-54. Interior looking west

△ **184-185** St Clement Danes, Strand, Westminster, 1680-82 upper stage of Tower 1719-20. Drawing; study for elevation, and **185** exterior from the west

186 Westminster Abbey. Drawing; elevation of North Transept, 1719

△ ▷ 187-189 Ingestre, Staffordshire, Church of St Mary, 1673-76. Exterior from the south-west. Interior looking east, and the pulpit.

△ **192** Marlborough House, St James's, London, 1709-11. Engraved by James Lightbody, *c* 1711

Venerande Pater;

Sententia apud antiquos vulgata est, quam ex ore tuo me habuisse memini, Parentibus nihil posse reddi æquivalens. Frequentes enim curæ, et perpetui labores circa pueros, sunt immensi quidem amoris indicium. At præcepta illa mihi toties repetita, quæ animum ad bonas Artes, & Virtutem impellunt, omnes alios amores superant. Quod meum est, efficiam, quantum potero, ne ingrato fiant hæc munera. Deus Optimus Maximus conatibus meis adsit, et Tibi, pro visceribus illis Paternæ pietatis, quæ maxime velis, præstet. Id orat.

Filius tuus

Tibi omni obsequio devotissimus

Christophorus Wren

△ **193** Letter from Wren to his father, January 1641. From *Parentalia* (Heirloom copy). *c* 1647

▽ **194** Design for a weather-clock *c* 1647, by Wren. From *Parentalia* (Heirloom copy)

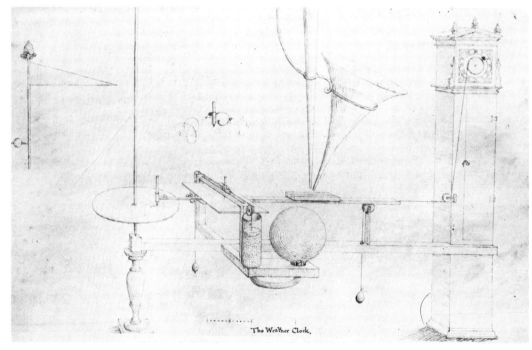

The Weather Clock.

(1.)

Oratio Inauguralis si
Habita Londini in Collegio Greshamen:
Per Chr. Wren A.M.
Astronomiæ Professorem, Electum
In Anno 1657, Ætat. 25.

Quanquam ex circumfusâ hac undique (Auditores Spectatissimi) tam Illustri coronâ felix admodum mihimet Augurium facio, facile exspectandum fore, germanam illam (quæ candidis Mathematicorum Pectoribus innata solet) Benevolentiam: ut ingenuè tamen quod sentio fatear, id mihi ut bene Invenio, sublimen Astronomiæ Cathedram hodiè conscendente quod in aëriâ Turris cujusdam specula positis accidit: quibus etiamsi nihil visum effugiat, sed integrum Cæli Fornicem (subjectæ Planitiei in finitore quasi incumbentem) prospicere detur, et pulcherrimâ longe latèq Rerum varietate afficiantur Oculi; Caligine tamen (ex inusitato Spectaculo) facile confunduntur: Neq mihi sanè (propter immensam Materiæ Copiam et altitudinem) satis in promptu est, quid imprimis, quid ultimò (in hoc minimè vulgari dicendi genere) vobis expediam. Quin ea est præterea harum Scientiarum pressa et benè morata Oratio quæ Rhetoricæ solutam Loquacitatem nullo

A.

195 The first page of Wren's inaugural
oration as Gresham Professor of Astronomy,
1657. From *Parentalia* (Heirloom copy)

△   **196** Sir Christopher Wren, 1632-1723.
Marble bust, *c* 1673 by Edward Pierce. For detail
see *Frontispiece*

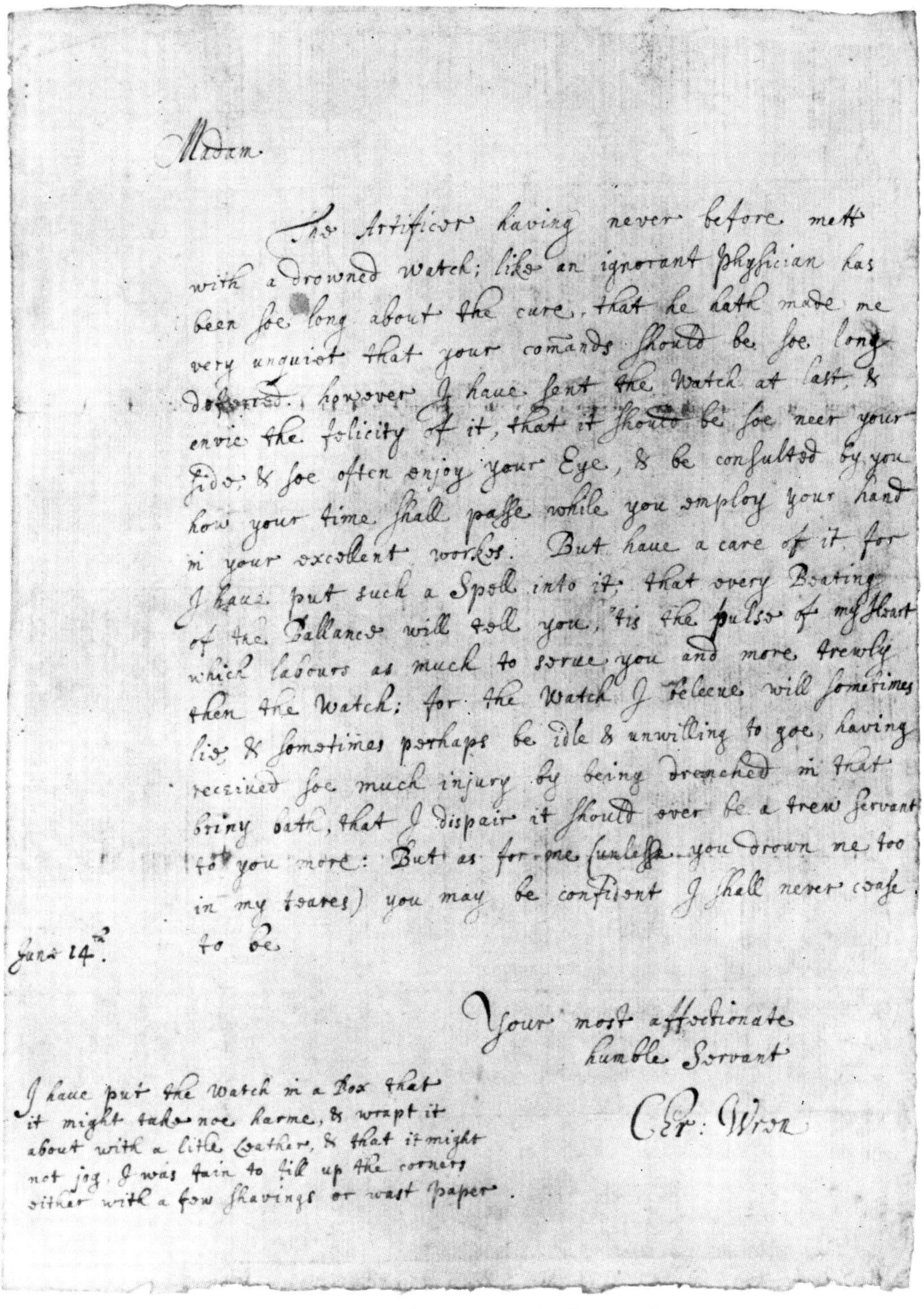

Madam

The Artificer having never before mett with a drowned watch; like an ignorant physician has been soe long about the cure, that he hath made me very unquiet that your comands should be soe long doferred. however I haue sent the Watch at last, & envie the felicity of it, that it should be soe neer your side, & soe often enjoy your Eye, & be consulted by you how your time shall passe while you employ your hand in your excelent workes. But haue a care of it, for I haue put such a Spell into it; that every Beating of the Ballance will tell you, 'tis the pulse of my Heart which labours as much to serue you and more truely then the Watch; for the Watch I beleeue will sometimes lie, & sometimes perhaps be idle & unwilling to goe, having received soe much injury by being drenched in that briny bath, that I dispair it should euer be a trew servant to you more: Butt as for me (unlesse you drown me too in my teares) you may be confident I shall never cease to be

June 14th.

Your most affectionate
humble Servant

Cꞅ: Wren

I haue put the Watch in a Box that
it might take noe harme, & wrapt it
about with a litle Leathers, & that it might
not jog, I was fain to fill up the corners
either with a few shavings or wast paper.

△ **197** Letter from Wren to his future wife, Faith Coghill, *c* 1668. From *Parentalia* (Heirloom copy)

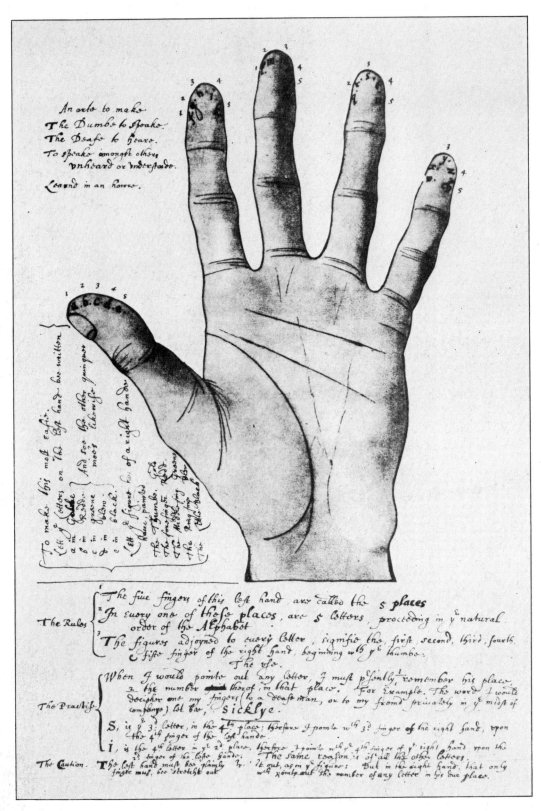

△ **198** Drawing of a hand by Wren inscribed 'An arte to make The Dumbe to speake. The Deafe to heare . . .'. From *Parentalia*, (Heirloom copy)

▷ **199** Sir Christopher Wren, 1632-1723. Painting by Antonio Verrio, Sir Godfrey Kneller and Sir James Thornhill, *c* 1706-24

c Tabulam invenit & incepit Anton: Verrio Perfecerunt Gothofredus Kneller & Joc: Thornhill Equ

△ **200** Sir Christopher Wren, 1632-1723. ▽ **201** Drawing by Henry Cooke, c 1683
Painting by Sir Godfrey Kneller, 1711

▷ **202** Sir Christopher Wren, 1632-1723.
Detail of painting by Sir Godfrey Kneller, 1711
(*see* pl. 200)

△ **203** Sir Christopher Wren, 1632-1723.
Portrait relief, ivory by David Le Marchand,
c 1723

△ **204** Jane Wren, 1678-1704. Marble relief,
St Paul's Cathedral, Crypt

△ **205** Christopher Wren, jnr, 1675-1747.
Engraved by Isaac Faber, 1750

▽ **206** Death Mask of Sir Christopher Wren, 1723

.SUBTUS CONDITUR
HUIUS ECCLESIÆ ET VRBIS CONDITOR
CHRISTOPHORUS WREN,
QUI VIXIT ANNOS ULTRA NONAGINTA,
NON SIBI SED BONO PUBLICO.
LECTOR, SI MONUMENTUM REQUIRIS,
CIRCUMSPICE.
Obijt XXV. Feb: An? MDCCXXIII. Æt.XCI.

△   **207** Tomb of Sir Christopher Wren,
1723. St Paul's Cathedral, Crypt

Bibliography

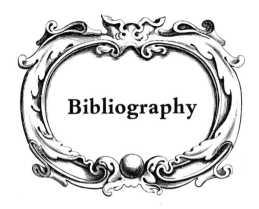

Bibliography

This list provides the reader with most of the relevant literature of the past 70 years on Wren's life and work. I have excluded short articles about the 1923 Bicentenary of death celebrations, the post-war restoration of the City churches, and those buildings proved in recent years to be by architects other than Wren.

Books

Beard G. *Craftsmen and Interior Decoration in England, 1660-1820.* Edinburgh: John Bartholomew & Son Ltd, 1981.

Birch GH. *London Churches of the Seventeenth and Eighteenth Centuries.* London: Batsford, 1896.

Bolton AT, Hendry HD, eds. *The Wren Society.* London: 1924-43: Volumes 1-20. Includes all known drawings, with exception of those formerly in the Bute collection (sold Sotheby's 23 May 1951). The following volumes deal in particular with St Paul's: Vol I (1924); Vol II (1925); III (1926); XII (1936); XIV (1937); XV (1938); XVI (1939). The detailed Index is in Vol XX (1943).

Briggs MS. *Christopher Wren.* London: Falcon Educational Books, 1951.

Idem. Wren, The Incomparable. London: Allen & Unwin, 1953.

Bumpus JS. *St Paul's Cathedral.* London: Treasure House Series, 1913.

Caröe WD, ed. *Tom Tower, Christ Church, Oxford: Some Letters of Sir Christopher Wren to John Fell, Bishop of Oxford.* Oxford: Clarendon Press, 1923.

Castells FdeP. *Was Sir Christopher Wren a Mason?* London: Kenning & Son, 1917.

Clarke BFL. *Parish Churches of London.* London: Batsford, 1966. Gives details of wartime destruction and post-war restoration.

Clayton J. *Plans, Elevations and Sections of the Parochial Churches of Sir Chr. Wren.* London: Longman & Co, 1849-49. The measured drawings were further reproduced in *Wren Society, Vol IX* (1932).

Cobb G. *The Old Churches of London.* London: Batsford, 1948: 3rd edn.

Idem. London City Churches. London: Batsford, 1977.

Colvin HM. *The Sheldonian Theatre and the Divinity School.* Oxford: OUP, 1974: 2nd edn.

Colvin HM, Crook JM, Downes K, Newman J. *The History of the King's Works, 1660-1782.* London: HMSO, 1976: **V.**

Colvin HM. *A Biographical Dictionary of British Architects, 1600-1840.* London: John Murray, 1978. It includes the best critical list of Wren's works.

Dean CGT. *The Royal Hospital, Chelsea.* London: Hutchinson, 1950.

Dircks R, ed. *Sir Christopher Wren 1632-1723.* London: RIBA, 1923. The RIBA Bicentenary Memorial Volume. It contains articles on various aspects of Wren's life and work.

Doumato L. *Sir Christopher Wren and St Paul's Cathedral.* Illinois: Vance Bibliographies, 1979. A bibliography in seven sections: Chronology; Work; Books by; Articles on; St Paul's Cathedral - books and articles; Miscellaneous.

Downes K. *English Baroque Architecture.* London: Zwemmer, 1966.

Idem. Christopher Wren. London: Allen Lane, 1971.

Idem. The Architecture of Wren. London: Granada, 1982.

Idem. Hawksmoor. London: Zwemmer, 1979: 2nd edn.

Dugdale Sir W, Ellis H. *The History of St Paul's Cathedral in London.* London: The Warren, 1818.

Dutton R. *The Age of Wren.* London: Batsford, 1951.

Elmes J. *Memoirs of the Life and Works of Sir Christopher Wren.* London: Priestley & Weale, 1823.

Evelyn J. *Diary.* De Beer E S, ed. Oxford: Clarendon Press, 1955: Vols 1-6.

Fürst V. *The Architecture of Sir Christopher Wren.* London: Lund Humphries, 1956.

Gotch J A. Sir Christopher Wren from the personal side. In: Dircks R, ed. *Op cit.*

Green D. *Grinling Gibbons: His Work as Carver and Statuary, 1648-1721.* London: Country Life. 1964.

Gunther R T, ed. *The Architecture of Sir Roger Pratt.* Oxford: Clarendon Press, 1928. Reprinted New York: Arno Press, 1979:

Harrison S E. *The Wren Screen from the Temple Church.* New York: Reprinted from *The Collector,* 1935.

Hooke R. *Diary 1672-80.* Robinson H W, Adams W, eds. London: Taylor & Francis, 1935.

Jarvis J. *Christopher Wren's Cotswold Masons.* Cheltenham: Thornhill Press, 1980.

Knoop D, Jones G P. *The London Mason in the Seventeenth Century.* Manchester: MUP, 1935.

Lang J. *Rebuilding St Paul's after the Great Fire of London.* Oxford: OUP, 1956.

Law E P. *The History of Hampton Court Palace.* London: G Bell & Sons, 1885-1891: Vols 1-3.

Lindsey J. *Wren, His Work and Times.* London: Rich & Cowan, 1951.

Little B D. *Sir Christopher Wren: a historical biography.* London: Robert Hale Ltd, 1975.

Longman W. *The History of the Three Cathedrals of St Paul's.* London: Longman, Green & Co, 1873.

Matthews W R *et al. A History of St Paul's Cathedral.* London: Phoenix House, 1957.

Milman H H. *Annals of St Paul's.* London: 1869: 2nd edn.

New E H. *Twenty Drawings of Sir Christopher Wren's Churches.* London: 1903.

Norman P. *The London City Churches.* London: London Society, 1929: 2nd edn.

Pearce E H. *Annals of Christ's Hospital.* London: Methuen & Co. 1908: 2nd edn.

Phillimore L. *Sir Christopher Wren: His Family and Times.* London: Kegan Paul & Co, 1881.

Poley A F E. *St Paul's Cathedral.* London: 1927. Printed privately for the author and depicts his measured drawings.

Reddaway T F. *The Rebuilding of London after the Great Fire.* London: Jonathan Cape, 1940.

Sekler E. *Wren and his place in European Architecture.* London: Faber, 1956.

Stringer G G, comp. *A Bibliography of Works about Sir Christopher Wren.* American Association of Architectural Bibliographers. University of Virginia Press, 1972; **IX** (Papers): 29-50.

Summerson Sir J. *Sir Christopher Wren* (Brief Lives Series No. 9). London: Collins, 1953; reissued 1965.

Idem. Architecture in Britain, 1530-1830 (Pelican History of Art Series) London: Penguin Books Ltd, 1963: **111**: 119-188; 4th edn.

Idem. The Sheldonian in its Time. Oxford: OUP, 1964. Pamphlet, reprinted from the *Oxford University Gazette* 1963 Dec 6.

Taylor A T. *The Towers and Steeples designed by Sir Christopher Wren.* London: Batsford, 1881.

Watkin D J, ed. *Sale Catalogues of Libraries of Eminent Persons.* London: Mansell Publishing/ Information Ltd & Sotheby Parke-Bernet Publications Ltd, 1972: **IV**: 1-43. The Wren Catalogue is also reprinted in Fürst V. *Op cit.*

Webb G. *Wren* (Great Lives Series). London: Duckworth, 1937.

Welch C. *The History of the Monument.* London: Committee for Letting the City's Lands, 1893.

Whinney M D, Millar O. *English Art, 1625-1714* (Oxford History of Art Series). Oxford: OUP, 1957: 204-232.

Whinney M D. *Wren.* London: Thames & Hudson, 1971.

Wren S. *Parentalia, or Memoirs of the Family of Wrens.* London: T Osborn & R Dodsley, 1750. The 'Heirloom Copy' is in the British Architectural Library and was reprinted as a facsimile edition in 1965. The section on Sir Christopher Wren was reprinted in an edition edited by E J Enthoven in 1903.

BIBLIOGRAPHY

Articles

Anon. Report on the Condition of St Paul's Cathedral by the Committee appointed by the Dean and Chapter. *Architectural Review* 1907; **22**: 107-125.

Anon. Six Wren Churches which are not to be rebuilt. *Architect's Journal* 1949 July 21; **110**: 65.

Anon. The Old Court House, Hampton Court: The home of N E Lamplugh Esquire (The last home of Sir Christopher Wren). *Architectural Review* 1923; **53**: 196-206.

Abercrombie P. Wren's Plan for London after the Great Fire. *Town Planning Review* 1923; **X**: 71-78.

Adshead S D. Sir Christopher Wren and his plan for London. In: Dircks R. ed. *Op cit.* (Books).

Allen W G, Peach C S. The Preservation of St Paul's. *RIBA Journal* 1930 Aug 9; **37**: 655-676.

Ascoli D. The Royal Hospital, Chelsea: a mystery. *Country Life* 1975 June 5; **157**: 1491-92.

Batten M I. Robert Hooke, a partner with Wren: discoveries in a diary (at Guildhall Library, London). *The Times* 1935 Feb 14; 13-14.

Beard G. Master Plasterers in the Age of Wren. *Country Life* 1973 Mar 22; **153**: 788-790.

Bennett J A. Wren's Last Building? *Notes and Records of the Royal Society* 1973: **XXVII**. (The Royal Society's Repository, *dem. c*1782).

Bennett J A. A Study of *Parentalia,* with two unpublished letters of Sir Christopher Wren. *Annals of Science* 1973; **XXX**: 129-147.

Bennett J A. Christopher Wren: Astronomy, Architecture and the Mathematical Sciences. *Journal for the History of Astronomy* 1975; **VI**.

Bennett J A. Hooke and Wren and the system of the World: some points towards an historical account. *British Journal for the History of Science* 1975; **8**: 32-36.

Benton G M. Wren and Burnham-on-Crouch, Essex. *Transactions Essex Archaeological Society* 1952; **24**: 162-163.

Bettey J H. The Supply of Stone for Rebuilding St Paul's Cathedral. *Archaeological Journal* 1971; **128**: 176-185.

Bolton A T. Sir Christopher Wren's Intended Baldicchino for St Paul's Cathedral: New Light on an Old Problem. *RIBA Journal* 1936 Apr 4; **43**: 593-594

Briggs M S. Wren's Castles in the Air; His Unrealised Schemes for Royal Palaces. *The Builder* 1951 Jan 12; **180**: 37-40.

Chancellor E B. Wren's Restoration of Westminster Abbey: The Drawings. *The Connoisseur* 1927; **78**: 145-147.

Chettle G H, Faulkner P A. Kensington Palace and Sir Christopher Wren: A Vindication. *Journal, British Archaeological Association* 1951; **XIV**: 1-14; 3rd Ser.

Clark S. Observations on Wren's System of Buttresses. In: Dircks R. ed. *Op cit.* (Books).

Cobb G. The Towers and Spires of Sir Christopher Wren. *The Builder* 1942 June 5; **162**: 487-489.

Cole J C. William Byrd, stone cutter and mason and his association with Sir Christopher Wren. *Oxoniensia* 1952; **14**: 63-74.

Colvin H M. Roger North and Sir Christopher Wren. *Architectural Review* 1951; **110**: 257-260; with a correction, *Ibid;* **110**: 340.

Colvin H M. Easton Neston Reconsidered. *Country Life* 1970 Oct 15; **148**: 968-971.

Colvin H M. The Church of St Mary Aldermary and its rebuilding after the Great Fire of London. *Architectural History* 1981; **24**: 24-31.

Cook A. Wren's Design for Winchester Palace, Hampshire. In: Colvin H M, Harris J. eds. *The Country Seat: Studies in the History of the British Country House presented to Sir John Summerson.* 1970:58-63.

Crook J M. William Burges and the completion of St Paul's *The Antiquaries Journal* 1980; **LX; II**: 285-307.

Davies J H V. The dating of the buildings of the Royal Hospital at Greenwich, *Archaeological Journal* 1956; **CXIII**: 126-136.

Davis E J. The Parish Churches of the City of London. *Journal, Royal Society of Arts* 1935; **83**: 895-915.

Dean C G T. Lord Ranelagh's house in Chelsea: an unrecorded work by Sir Christopher Wren. *Transactions London and Middlesex Archaeological Society* 1935; N S **7**: 210-217.

Downes K. Wren and Whitehall in 1664. *Burlington Magazine* 1971; **113**: 89-92.

Esdaile K. The so-called aged Wren (portrait). *Architectural Review* 1944; **95**: 142-143.

Farquharson J, MacDonald C. Greenwich Hospital and Sir Christopher Wren's Designs, *Architectural Review* 1911; **29**: 3-12; 77-83.

Feilden B, Caring for St Paul's. *RIBA Journal* 1971: 490-493.

Fisher H A L. The Real Oxford Movement. From: *Pages from the Past* 1939. (Wren and his circle at Oxford).

Fletcher H M. Sir Christopher Wren's Carpentry; a Note on the Library at Trinity College, Cambridge. *RIBA Journal* 1923; **XXX:** 388; 3rd Ser.

Freeman A. Renatus Harris's proposed St Paul's organ and his puzzling invention (*c* 1712.) *Organ* 1930: 74-77.

Furniss L. A Comparison: Two Reputed Houses of Sir Christopher Wren. *Architectural Review* 1907; **21:** 15-21.

George R E G. St Paul's Cathedral: Influence of Bernini and the Baroque Tradition on Wren's Work. *Quarterly Review* 1942; 52-62.

Halley J M W. The Rebuilding and the Workmen of St Paul's Cathedral from the Accounts. *RIBA Journal* 1915; **XXII;** 3rd Ser.

Hamilton S B. The Place of Sir Christopher Wren in the History of Structural Engineering. *Newcomen Society, Transactions* 1933-34; **14:** 27-42.

Harris J. Cast Iron Columns, 1706, in the House of Commons. *Architectural Review* 1961; **130:** 60-61.

Harvey P D A. A Signed Plan by Sir Christopher Wren. *British Museum Quarterly* 1962; **25:** 66-69.

Hope R. Doorway by Wren at Lord Weymouth's School (Warminster). *Architectural Review* 1966; **139:** 478-479.

Highfield J R L. Alexander Fisher, Sir Christopher Wren and Merton College Chapel. *Oxoniensia* 1960; **24:** 70-82.

Huxley G H. The Geometrical Work of Sir Christopher Wren. *Scripta Mathematica* 1960; **XXV.**

Jones H W. Sir Christopher Wren and Natural Philosophy: with a check list of his scientific activities. *Notes and Records of the Royal Society* 1958; **XIII.**

Keen A. The Ceilings of the City Churches. *Architectural Review* 1911; **29:** 68-76; 136-143.

Keen A. Sir Christopher Wren's Parish Churches. In: Dircks R, ed. *Op cit* (Books).

Kimball F. Wren: Some of His Sources. *Architectural Review* 1924; **55:** 90-96.

Law W T. Notes on the Wren Pedigree. *Genealogist* 1889; N S **VI:** 168-171.

Leacroft R. Wren's Drury Lane. *Architectural Review* 1950; **110:** 43-46.

Lynton N. A Wren drawing for St Paul's *Burlington Magazine* 1955; **97:** 40-44; Reply by Sir John Summerson, *Ibid;* **97:** 120.

Macartney M E. Some Recent Investigations at St Paul's. In: Dircks R, ed. *Op cit* (Books).

Minns E H, Webb M. Pembroke College Chapel, Sir Christopher Wren's First Building. In: Dircks R, ed. *Op cit* (Books).

Oswald A. Winslow Hall, Bucks - 'one of the very few country houses that can confidently be attributed to Sir Christopher Wren'. *Country Life* 1951 Aug 24: 572-576.

Paget J C. Wren's Reputed House on Botolph Lane. *Architectural Review* 1906; **19:** 147-154.

Pevsner N. Sir Christopher Wren (his early life as scientist and later as architect of London City Churches). *Proceedings, Royal Institution of Great Britain* 1956; **35/4; 161:** 734-739.

Pite A B. The design of St Paul's Cathedral. In: Dircks R, ed. *Op cit* (Books).

Reddaway T F. Sir Christopher Wren's Navy Office. *Bulletin of the Institute of Historical Research* 1957; **XXX:** 175-188.

Richardson A R. Sir Christopher Wren's Public Buildings. In: Dircks R, ed. *Op cit* (Books).

Smallwood F T. Did Wren design Terrace House, Battersea?. The story of a notion. *Transactions London and Middlesex Archaeological Society* 1969; **22:** 33-38.

Smith H S. Pedigree of Wren. *The Genealogist* 1884; N S **i:** 262-266.

Stimson D. Evidence for Wren's greatness as reflected in his achievements in science. *Science Monthly* New York, 1941; 360-367.

Stratton A. Dutch Influences on the Architecture of Sir Christopher Wren. In: Dircks R, ed. *Op cit* (Books).

Stringer G G, comp. Bibliography of works about Sir Christopher Wren. *American Association of Architectural Bibliographers* 1972; **9:** 29-50.

Summerson Sir J. The Tyranny of the Intellect: A Study of the Mind of Sir Christopher Wren in Relation to the Thought of his Time. *RIBA Journal* 1937 Feb 20; 373-390; reprinted in author's *Heavenly Mansions and Other Essays on Architecture* London: Cresset Press, 1949.

Summerson Sir J. Christopher Wren at Work. Early studies and drawings of St Paul's Cathedral. *The Times* 1951 Oct 11.

Summerson Sir J. Drawings for the London City churches. *RIBA Journal* 1952: **59:** 126-129; 3rd Ser: with a reply by W W Scott-Moncrieff. *Ibid;* **59:** 187.

Summerson Sir J. Sir Christopher Wren, PRS. In: Hartley H, ed. *The Royal Society: its Origin and Founders* 1960: 99-105.

Summerson Sir J. The Penultimate Design for St Paul's. *Burlington Magazine* 1961; **CIII:** 83-89.

Summerson Sir J. Drawings of London churches in the Bute Collections: a catalogue. *Architectural History* 1970; **XIII:**30-42.

Tanner L E. Wren's Restoration of Westminster Abbey; the signatures. *The Connoisseur* 1927; **LXXVIII.**

Thomas A H *et al.* Sir Christopher Wren's descendants. *Notes and Queries* 1934 Oct 20: 277; Nov 10: 338.

Ward W H. French and Italian Influences on Sir Christopher Wren's Work. In: Dircks R, ed. *Op cit* (Books).

Warren E P. Sir Christopher Wren's Repair of the Divinity School and Duke Humphrey's Library. In: Dircks R, ed. *Op cit* (Books).

Weaver Sir L. The Interleaved Copy of Wren's *Parentalia* with Manuscript Insertions. *RIBA Journal* 1910-11; **18:** 569-585.

Whinney M D. Sir Christopher Wren's Visit to Paris (with French summary). *Gazette des Beaux-Arts* 1958; **LI:** 229-242.

Wilton-Ely J. The Architectural Model: English Baroque. *Apollo* 1968; **88:** 252-259.

Wright O. Greenwich Layout. *Architectural Review* 1960; **127:** 344-346.

Thesis

Bennett J A. Studies in the life and work of Sir Christopher Wren. *Cambridge PhD* 1976.

Location Map:
The London
City Churches

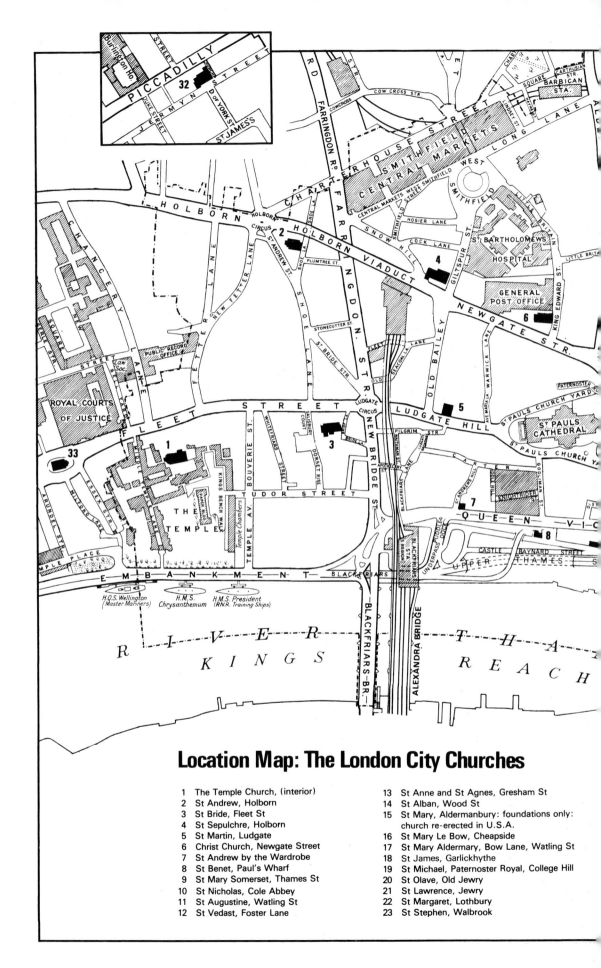

Location Map: The London City Churches

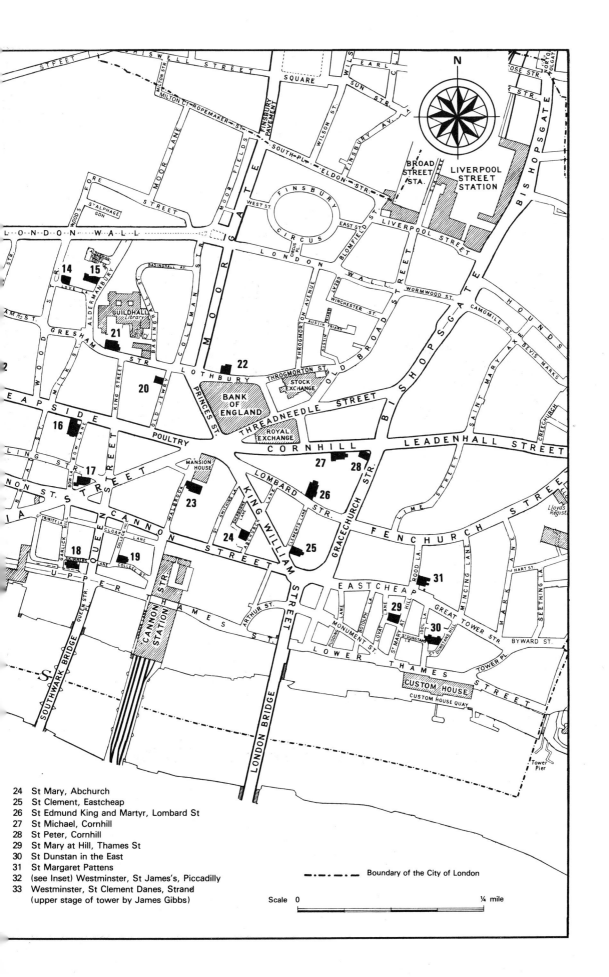

-·-·-·-·-·- Boundary of the City of London

Scale 0   ¼ mile

Plan of
St Paul's
Cathedral

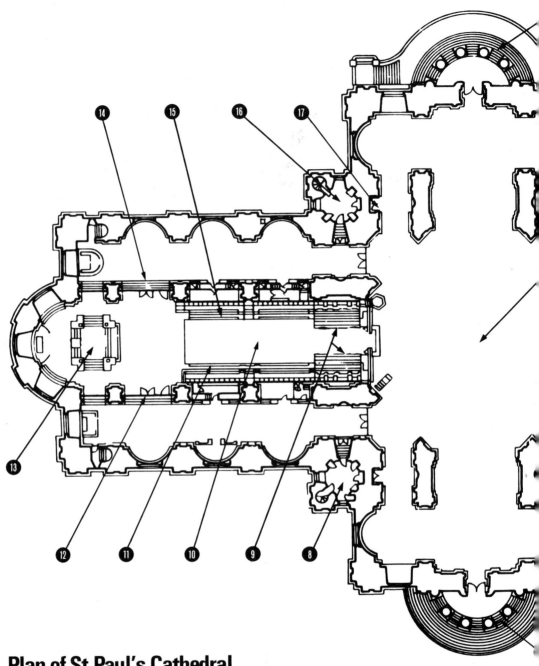

Plan of St Paul's Cathedral

Key to Plan

1 West front. See pls 73,93,103.
2 North West Tower. See pls 74,93,102,109.
3 Morning Prayer Chapel
4 Nave. See pl 128.
5 The Lord Mayor's Vestry
6 One of the eight piers (at the entrance to the North

Transept) supporting the Dome. See pl 129.
7 The North Portico. See pls 77,106
8 The Canon's Vestry
9 The Organ. See pls 110,111, 125,130.
10 The Choir. See pls 110, 111, 125,130-132.
11 Choir Stalls, North Side.

See pls 110, 122-125.
12 Jean Tijou's Wrought Iron Gates, North side of Choir. See pls 120,133.
13 The High Altar. See pl 128 (dest. 1940); The High Altar and Baldacchino (1958) see pl 130.
14 Jean Tijou's Wrought

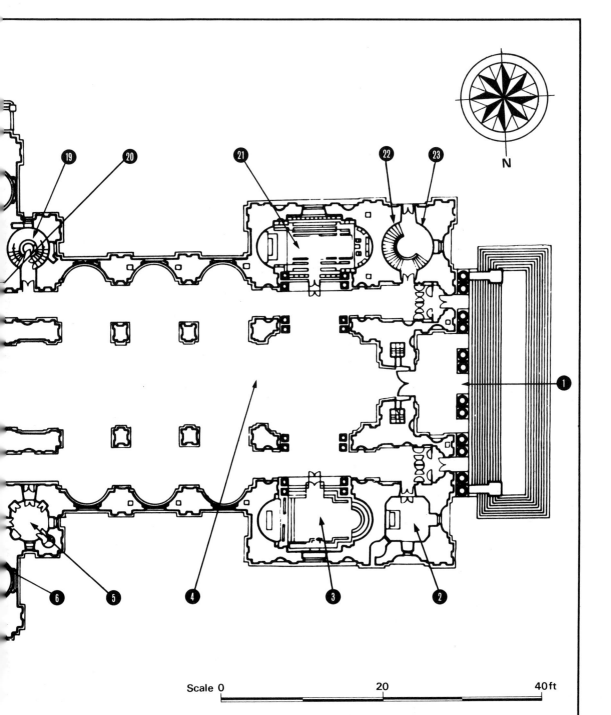

Scale 0   20   40 ft

Index

Index